REVISE AQA GCSE (9-1) English Language

GUIDED REVISION WORKBOOK

Series Consultant: Harry Smith

Authors: Mark Roberts and Charlotte Woolley

Also available to support your revision:

Revise GCSE Study Skills Guide   9781447967071

The **Revise GCSE Study Skills Guide** is full of tried-and-trusted hints and tips for how to learn more effectively. It gives you techniques to help you achieve your best — throughout your GCSE studies and beyond!

Revise GCSE Revision Planner   9781447967828

The **Revise GCSE Revision Planner** helps you to plan and organise your time, step-by-step, throughout your GCSE revision. Use this book and wall chart to mastermind your revision.

> **For the full range of Pearson revision titles across KS2, KS3, GCSE, Functional Skills, AS/A Level and BTEC visit:**
> www.pearsonschools.co.uk/revise

Contents

SECTION A: READING
1. The exam papers explained
2. Planning your exam time
3. Paper 1 Reading questions 1
4. Paper 1 Reading questions 2
5. Paper 2 Reading questions 1
6. Paper 2 Reading questions 2
7. Skimming for the main idea
8. Annotating the sources
9. Putting it into practice
10. Putting it into practice
11. The writer's viewpoint
12. Fact, opinion and expert evidence
13. Explicit information and ideas
14. Implicit information and ideas
15. Inference
16. Point–Evidence–Explain
17. Putting it into practice
18. Putting it into practice
19. Word classes
20. Connotations
21. Figurative language
22. Creation of character
23. Creating atmosphere
24. Narrative voice
25. Putting it into practice
26. Putting it into practice
27. Rhetorical devices 1
28. Rhetorical devices 2
29. Whole text structure: fiction
30. Whole text structure: non-fiction
31. Identifying sentence types
32. Commenting on sentences
33. Putting it into practice
34. Putting it into practice
35. Evaluating a fiction text 1
36. Evaluating a fiction text 2
37. Using evidence to evaluate
38. Putting it into practice
39. Writing about two texts
40. Selecting evidence for synthesis
41. Answering a synthesis question
42. Looking closely at language
43. Planning to compare language
44. Comparing language
45. Comparing structure
46. Comparing ideas
47. Comparing perspective
48. Answering a comparison question
49. Putting it into practice

SECTION B: WRITING
50. Writing questions: an overview
51. Writing questions: Paper 1
52. Writing questions: Paper 2
53. Writing questions: time management
54. Writing for a purpose: creative 1
55. Writing for a purpose: creative 2
56. Writing for a purpose: viewpoint 1
57. Writing for a purpose: viewpoint 2
58. Writing for an audience
59. Putting it into practice
60. Putting it into practice
61. Form: articles
62. Form: letters and reports
63. Form: speeches
64. Putting it into practice
65. Ideas and planning: creative
66. Structure: creative
67. Beginnings and endings: creative
68. Putting it into practice
69. Ideas and planning: viewpoint 1
70. Ideas and planning: viewpoint 2
71. Openings: viewpoint
72. Conclusions: viewpoint
73. Putting it into practice
74. Paragraphing
75. Linking ideas
76. Putting it into practice
77. Formality and standard English 1
78. Formality and standard English 2
79. Vocabulary for effect: synonyms
80. Vocabulary for effect: creative
81. Vocabulary for effect: viewpoint
82. Language for different effects 1
83. Language for different effects 2
84. Language for different effects 3
85. Putting it into practice
86. Putting it into practice
87. Sentence variety 1
88. Sentence variety 2
89. Sentences for different effects
90. Putting it into practice
91. Ending a sentence
92. Commas
93. Apostrophes and speech punctuation
94. Colons, semi-colons, dashes, brackets and ellipses
95. Putting it into practice
96. Common spelling errors 1
97. Common spelling errors 2
98. Common spelling errors 3
99. Proofreading
100. Putting it into practice

SOURCES
101. Source 1 – *Rebecca*
102. Source 2 – *The Kite Runner*
103. Source 3 – 'The Yellow Wallpaper'
104. Source 4 – 'There Will Come Soft Rains'
105. Source 5a – 'Googled your cough?'
106. Source 5b – 'The Boat to America'
107. Source 6a – 'Women aren't "better" at housework – but men sure are better at avoiding it'
108. Source 6b – *The American Frugal Housewife*
109. Source 7a – 'Creating ghost stories'
110. Source 7b – 'Haunted Houses'

111 PRACTICE PAPERS

120 ANSWERS

A small bit of small print

AQA publishes Sample Assessment Material and the Specification on its website. This is the official content and this book should be used in conjunction with it. The questions in this book have been written to help you practise what you have learned in your revision. Remember: the real exam questions may not look like this.

Had a go ☐   Nearly there ☐   Nailed it! ☐

SECTION A READING

The exam papers explained

The English Language GCSE is split into two exam papers:
- Paper 1: Explorations in creative reading and writing
- Paper 2: Writers' viewpoints and perspectives

Each paper has a reading section (Section A) and a writing section (Section B). Remind yourself of the content of each exam then answer the questions that follow.

Paper 1, Section A: Reading	**Paper 1, Section B: Writing**
You will be asked to read one fiction text from the 20th or 21st century that will be approximately 500–800 words long. You will be asked four questions that will test your understanding of the text.	You will be asked to write a descriptive or narrative piece of writing from a choice of two. One of the questions will have a visual stimulus to help you generate ideas.

Paper 2, Section A: Reading	**Paper 2, Section B: Writing**
You will be asked to read one non-fiction text and one non-literary text – these will be drawn from the 19th century, and either the 20th or 21st century. You will be asked four questions that will test your understanding of the text.	You will be asked to write a text for a particular target audience on a theme that will have been introduced in the reading section.

 1 (a) Which paper asks you to read a fiction text? ....

(b) Which paper and section ask you to use a visual stimulus? ....

(c) What should you do in the first 15 minutes of an exam? ....

(d) Which question gives you a choice? ....

(e) How many questions will you be asked to complete for each exam? ....

(f) Which paper asks you to read non-fiction texts? ....

> As well as ensuring that you revise thoroughly, it's also vital you plan effectively for the exam day itself by ensuring that you are physically and mentally prepared.

2 Think about each text type below. State if it is useful preparation for Paper 1 or Paper 2.

Text type	Paper 1 or 2?	Text type	Paper 1 or 2?
(a) Report		(h) Novel ending	
(b) Short story		(i) Diary	
(c) Biography		(j) Novel opening	
(d) Middle of a novel		(k) Travelogue	
(e) Opening of a short story		(l) Essay	
(f) Newspaper article		(m) Description of character or setting	
(g) Letter			

SECTION A READING

Had a go ☐   Nearly there ☐   Nailed it! ☐

Planning your exam time

Time management is a vital part of being successful in your exams. Using your time effectively, including reading time and allocating the correct amount of time per question, will help you to show off your skills and maximise your chances of getting the result you deserve.

> Work out how long you should spend on each question according to the number of marks it is worth, for example, a 4-mark question should take approximately 4 minutes to complete. You have got 15 minutes reading time within the **total** time allocation for each paper. Read the questions first to get a sense of when you should spend time reading for each question.

Guided

1 Use your 15 minutes reading time productively. Number the following statements from 1 to 6 to show the order you think will be most effective:

A Skim read the sources so you understand the main themes. ☐

B Annotate the sources with brief notes that relate to the question. ☐

C Read the questions before you read the sources so you know what to look for and what to read when. ☐

D Read the sources, especially the introduction as it will give you important clues about the genre, context and audience. ☐

E Use highlighters to identify key quotations to come back to, but be careful to make sure you only highlight relevant sections. ☐

F For questions with line numbers, make a quick mark beside the relevant line on the source. ☐

2 Complete the table below by working out how much time you could spend on each question.

Paper 1		Marks allocated	Time I should spend
	Reading time		15 minutes
Section A: Reading	Q1	4	
	Q2	8	8 minutes
	Q3	8	
	Q4	20	
Section B: Writing	Planning time		5 minutes
	Q5	40	
	Checking my answers		5 minutes
		Total time:	1 hour 45 minutes

Paper 2		Marks allocated	Time I should spend
	Reading time		15 minutes
Section A: Reading	Q1	4	
	Q2	8	8 minutes
	Q3	12	
	Q4	16	
Section B: Writing	Planning time		5 minutes
	Q5	40	
	Checking my answers		5 minutes
		Total time:	1 hour 45 minutes

Had a go ☐ Nearly there ☐ Nailed it! ☐

SECTION A READING

Paper 1 Reading questions 1

It is important that you understand how each question is being assessed. The examiner will have a specific mark scheme that will be used to decide on the mark for your answer.

In **Paper 1, Section A: Reading Question 1**, you are assessed for:

Assessment objective 1
(a) Identify and interpret explicit and implicit information and ideas
(b) Select and synthesise evidence from different texts

Paper 1

1 Read the exam-style question below. **You don't need to answer it.** Instead, identify which part of assessment objective 1 the question tests. Circle your choice.

1 Read again the first part of **source 10, lines 1 to 20**.
List **four** reasons why the children dislike visiting Mrs Dubose. **(4 marks)**

This question tests: AO1(a)   AO1(b)

> Question 1 will direct you to a specific part of the source and ask you to select specific information – there is no need for a detailed analysis.
> You do not get extra marks for finding implicit information in the text. If there are four pieces of explicit information, you can use these for quick marks.

In **Paper 1, Section A: Reading Question 2**, you are assessed for:

Assessment objective 2
Explain, comment on and analyse how writers use language and structure to achieve effects and influence readers, using relevant subject terminology to support their views

Paper 1

2 Read the exam-style question below. **You don't need to answer it.**

2 Look in detail at this extract from **lines 22 to 32** of the source.
How does the writer use language here to reveal the children's fear of Mrs Dubose?
You could include the writer's choice of:
- words and phrases
- language features and techniques
- sentence forms. **(8 marks)**

> Question 2 will direct you to a specific part of the source and ask you for a longer answer that refers to the way a writer uses **language** to create particular effects.

(a) Circle the key information in the question.

(b) How long should you spend on this question? ....

3 Which assessment focus would you expect the following exam-style questions to be assessed on? Circle your choice.

(a) How does the writer use language to help generate excitement in the text?
AO1(a)   AO1(b)   AO2

(b) Identify four aspects of Mrs Dubose's character.
AO1(a)   AO1(b)   AO2

SECTION A READING

Had a go ☐ Nearly there ☐ Nailed it! ☐

Paper 1 Reading questions 2

For Question 3 and Question 4 in **Paper 1, Section A: Reading**, it is important that you produce a developed, analytical response that reveals your understanding of the writer at work.

In **Paper 1, Section A: Reading Question 3**, you are assessed for:

Assessment objective 2

Explain, comment on and analyse how writers use language and structure to achieve effects and influence readers, using relevant subject terminology to support their views

Read the exam-style question below. **You don't need to answer it.**

Paper 1

3 You now need to think about the **whole** of the **source**.
   This text is taken from the opening of a novel.
   How has the writer structured the text to interest you as a reader?
   You could write about:
   • what the writer focuses your attention on at the beginning
   • how and why the writer changes this focus as the extract develops
   • any other structural features that interest you. **(8 marks)**

> Question 3 will ask you to refer to the whole of the source and comment on how the writer has used structure to create particular effects on the reader.

1 Tick the statements that you think apply to the question:
   A I don't need to use evidence to support my analysis.
   B I should comment on structure.
   C I should spend approximately 8 minutes on this question.
   D I should refer to the writer at work.
   E I need to use comparison skills to answer this question.
   F I need to consider the impact of the text on the reader.

In **Paper 1, Section A: Reading Question 4**, you are assessed for:

Assessment objective 4

Evaluate texts critically and support this with appropriate textual references

> Question 4 will ask you to refer to a particular section from the source and assesses your ability to evaluate the impact of the text on the reader. You are also encouraged to provide a personal response to the question, using textual evidence to support your analysis.

Read the exam-style question below. **You don't need to answer it.**

Paper 1

4 Focus this part of your answer on the second half of the source, from **lines 29 to 51**.
   A student, having read this section of the text, said: 'The narrator doesn't seem to take any responsibility for what happened.'
   To what extent do you agree?
   In your response, you could:
   • write about your own impression of the narrator's involvement in the incident
   • evaluate how the writer presents the narrator's involvement
   • support your opinions with quotations from the text. **(20 marks)**

2 Circle the statements that you think apply to this question:

My personal opinion is not allowed.   I need to use evidence to support my analysis.
I should refer to the whole of the source. I should refer to a specific section of the source.
I should spend 20 minutes on the question. I need to evaluate the text critically.

Had a go ☐ Nearly there ☐ Nailed it! ☐

SECTION A READING

Paper 2 Reading questions 1

There are a variety of question types in Paper 2, which also include a comparison of texts.
In **Paper 2, Section A: Reading Questions 1 and 2**, you are assessed for:

Assessment objective 1
(a) Identify and interpret explicit and implicit information and ideas
(b) Select and synthesise evidence from different texts

> In Question 1, you will be directed to a specific part of the source and there will be some true and false statements listed. It is important that you carefully consider each possible statement and only shade the number of boxes you have been asked to shade.

Read the exam-style questions below. **You do not need to answer them.** Then answer the questions at the bottom of the page.
Question 1 has been completed by a student.

1 Read again **source 6b, lines 1 to 8**. Choose four statements below which are TRUE.
   • Shade the boxes of the ones that you think are true.
   • Choose a maximum of four statements.
   A It is worth spending the time to make things.
   B Cotton is more expensive than wool.
   C Knitted stockings are better than woven stockings.
   D The writer enjoys being organised and planning things.
   E Children or old people don't need to help around the house.
   F Saving money is a skill.
   G Some things are so cheap to buy that there is no point making them.
   H The writer thinks that money is more important than time.

   (4 marks)

> In Question 2 you will be asked to refer to two sources and you select relevant evidence from both sources to support your ideas.

2 You need to refer to **source 6a** and **source 6b** for this question.
   Use details from **both** sources.
   Write a summary of how both writers present illness.   **(8 marks)**

1 (a) Which question is asking you to make links between two texts? ....

   (b) How long should you spend on Question 1? ....

   (c) How long should you spend on Question 2? ....

   (d) Which question is asking you to focus on a part of the source? ....

   (e) How do you show your answer to Question 1? ....

   (f) Where has the student gone wrong in answering Question 1? ....

   (g) Which question is asking you to synthesise? ....

> 'To synthesise' means 'to bring together details from **both** texts into a written summary'.

SECTION A READING

Had a go ☐ Nearly there ☐ Nailed it! ☐

Paper 2 Reading questions 2

In **Paper 2, Section A: Reading Question 3**, you are assessed for:

Assessment objective 2
Explain, comment on and analyse how writers use language and structure to achieve effects and influence readers, using relevant subject terminology to support their views

> You will be asked a question on the 19th-century source and will be expected to refer to the whole of the extract.

1. Read the exam-style question below. **You don't need to answer it**. Instead, annotate the question to show the following information:
   - how many texts you need to refer to
   - how much of the text you need to use
   - which are the key words
   - how long to spend on writing an answer.

Paper 2

3. You now need to refer (only to source 6b.)
   How does the writer use language to express her viewpoint on housekeeping? **(12 marks)**

   — One text

In **Paper 2, Section A: Reading Question 4**, you are assessed for:

Assessment objective 3
Compare writers' ideas and perspectives, as well as how they are conveyed, across two or more texts

2. (a) Read the exam-style question below. The table shows one student's planning for the question where they have found evidence for each of the bullet points. Write the bullet points in the correct place in column 1 of the table.

Paper 2

4. For this question, you need to refer to the **whole of source 6a** together with **source 6b**.
   Compare how the two writers convey their different attitudes towards housework.
   In your answer, you could:
   - compare their different attitudes
   - compare the methods they use to convey their attitudes
   - support your ideas with quotations from both texts. **(16 marks)**

In your answer, you could:	6a 'Women aren't "better" at housework' (21st century)	6b *The American Frugal Housewife* (19th century)
	Housework is boring	Make sure nothing – food nor money – is wasted
	Angry and frustrated	Dedicated and organised
	Colloquial language	Use of imperatives

(b) Annotate the exam-style Question 4 in the same way as you did for exam-style Question 3 above, using the bullet points listed in Question 1.

6

Had a go ☐   Nearly there ☐   Nailed it! ☐

SECTION A READING

Skimming for the main idea

Look at this short extract from **source 5a**, 'Googled your cough?', then answer the questions below. The first one has been done for you.

> **'Googled your cough? Is death now upon you?'**
> At 11am I had a strange pain in my toe. By 11.05 I was convinced it was a brain tumour. By 11.15 I'd realised that, actually, my shoes were probably to blame, but by that time I'd already decided on the music that should be played at my funeral.

1. What does the headline suggest about the main idea or theme of the article?

   The headline suggests that the main idea of the article is that researching injuries or illnesses makes you worry.

2. What do the opening sentences suggest about the main idea or theme of the article?

   The opening sentences suggest that the main idea of the article is that researching injuries or illnesses makes you worry, although it also suggests ....

   ....

Now read these sentences from the end of the same article, then answer the questions below.

> Indeed, it's possible that, by now, you are starting to remember that your toe hurts, or you have a headache, or your leg is twitching. You may feel an urge to Google your symptoms. Hypochondriacs, please proceed with caution.

3. What does the end suggest about the article's main idea or theme?

   The end of the article suggests that looking up your health symptoms online is ....

   ....

4. Do the ideas expressed at the end of the article differ from those you found at the beginning?

   ....

   ....

> Skim reading a text can give you a good idea of what it is about before you read it more closely. Look at:
> - the headline, title or headings
> - the first sentence of each paragraph
> - the last sentence of the text.

Turn to the full article, 'Googled your cough?', on page 105. Skim read it for 30 seconds, then answer Question 5.

5. In one sentence, sum up the main idea in the article as a whole. Choose some of the words listed below to help you.

   anxiety   searching   diagnose   tempted   imagine   careful

   ....

   ....

   ....

   ....

7

SECTION A READING

Had a go ☐ Nearly there ☐ Nailed it! ☐

Annotating the sources

Read this short annotated extract from **source 1**, *Rebecca* by Daphne Du Maurier. The narrator is describing returning to her house, called Manderley.

> There was Manderley, our Manderley, secretive and silent as it had always been, the grey stone shining in the moonlight of my dream. [...] Time could not wreck the perfect symmetry of those walls, nor the site itself, a jewel in the hollow of a hand. **The terrace sloped to the lawns, and the lawns stretched to the sea, and turning I could see the sheet of silver placid under the moon, like a lake undisturbed by wind or storm. I turned again to the house, and though it stood inviolate[1], untouched, as though we ourselves had left but yesterday, I saw that the garden had obeyed the jungle law, even as the woods had done.**

1: inviolate: injury-free

A Sibilant adjectives, suggesting a sense of eerie stillness.

B Simile indicates stillness, and a place of value.

C Long sentence highlights the flowing, dreamlike quality of the experience.

D Repetition of the house name — could be comforting, or a threat, as it has its own character.

Now read this exam-style question. **You don't need to answer it**. Instead, think about what it is asking you to do, then answer the questions that follow.

Paper 1

2 Look in detail at **lines 7 to 15** of the source.
   How does the writer use language here to create an unsettling atmosphere around the house?
   You could include the writer's choice of:
   • words and phrases
   • language features and techniques
   • sentence forms.
   (8 marks)

Read the section in bold from the end of the extract.

1 Identify three places where there is a sense of an unsettling atmosphere:

   Word/phrase: .... Technique: ....

   Word/phrase: .... Technique: ....

   Word/phrase: .... Technique: ....

> Look for language features and techniques including verbs, similes, metaphors or contrasts.
> You could also look for individual words that create an unsettled feel.

2 For each of the three words or phrases you have identified, explain briefly why they create an unsettling atmosphere. Use the sentence openers below, or write your own.

   It suggests an ....

   There is a sense of ....

   The reader infers that ....

> You could use vocabulary like: 'contrasting'; 'unexpected'; 'untamed'; 'eerie'; 'unnatural calm'; 'threat'; 'unnerving'.

Had a go ☐   Nearly there ☐   Nailed it! ☐

SECTION A READING

Putting it into practice

 Read the full extract from **source 4**, 'There Will Come Soft Rains' on page 104, then answer Questions 1 and 2 below.

1 (a) Highlight, circle or underline any words or phrases in the extract from 'There Will Come Soft Rains' that would help you to answer the exam-style question below.

> You could look for:
> - personification
> - verb choices
> - repetition
> - use of time or numbers
> - use of sound.
>
> Other things might also catch your attention.

2 Look in detail at **lines 4 to 16** of the source.
How does the writer use language here effectively to describe the atmosphere in the house?
You could include the writer's choice of:
- words and phrases
- language features and techniques
- sentence forms.

(8 marks)

(b) Make notes about the effect that each word or phrase you have identified has on the reader.

'hissing sigh' – personification and sibilance, suggests a tiredness or maybe something threatening.

We know how many people are in the house because ....

....

Repetition of time 'eight-one, tick-tock', is eerie and suggests ....

....

....

....

2 Now use your annotations and notes from Question 1 to write the first two paragraphs of an answer to the exam-style Question 2.

> When you tackle this kind of question in the exam, remember to:
> - spend about 8 minutes on your answer
> - highlight key words in the question so that you get the focus right
> - use only the lines of the text referred to in the question.

Bradbury creates a curious, but threatening atmosphere ....

....

....

....

....

> **Remember:** You are only being asked to write part of an answer on this page. In the exam, you will be given more space to write a full answer.

Putting it into practice

Read the full extract from *The American Frugal Housewife*, in **source 6b** on page 108, then answer Questions 1 and 2 below.

1 (a) Highlight, circle or underline any words or phrases in the extract that would help you to answer the exam-style question below.

Paper 2

> 3 You now need to refer **only** to **source 6b**.
> How does the writer use language to present their attitude towards money? **(12 marks)**

(b) Make notes about the effect that each word or phrase you have identified has on the reader. An example has been done for you.

'every member should be employed either in earning or saving money' – 'every' suggests that all members of the family should contribute.

....
....
....
....
....

Guided

2 Now use your annotations and notes from Question 1 to write the first two paragraphs of an answer to the exam-style Question 3.

> When you tackle this kind of question in the exam, remember to:
> - spend about 12 minutes on your answer
> - highlight key words in the question so that you get the focus right
> - focus on the way the ideas and point of view are expressed by the writer.

....
....
....
....
....
....
....
....
....
....

> **Remember**: You are only being asked to write part of an answer on this page. In the exam, you will be given more space to write a full answer.

Had a go ☐ Nearly there ☐ Nailed it! ☐

SECTION A READING

The writer's viewpoint

Below are extracts from the source materials for Paper 2 that can be found on pages 101–110. Briefly indicate what you think the writer's viewpoint is on the topic they are discussing. Some examples have been completed for you.

> Being able quickly to establish the viewpoint of the writer is vital to developing a secure understanding of the reading texts for Paper 2.

Topic 1: Sickness

Source 5a: from 'Googled your cough? Is death now upon you?'
Indeed, it's possible that, by now, you are starting to remember that your toe hurts, or you have a headache, or your leg is twitching.

Writer feels that thinking about health is likely to make the reader feel paranoid about becoming ill.

Source 5b: from 'The Boat to America'
Two passengers' wives (one of them my own) lay already in silent agonies on the sofa…

Writer has sympathetic attitude towards the passengers who feel sick.

Topic 2: Housework

Source 6a: from 'Women aren't "better" at housework – but men sure are better at avoiding it'
The more we all let men get away with saying that they just 'don't care' about filth […] the longer the chore disparity will last.

....
....

Source 6b: from *The American Frugal Housewife*
Buy merely enough to get along with at first. It is only by experience that you can tell what will be the wants of your family.

....
....

Topic 3: Haunted places

Source 7a: from 'Creating ghost stories'
You walk in an ancient forest and some of the weathered and pollarded[4] trees have grown into odd shapes. Often, with a little imagination, those trees can show faces, distorted like gargoyles or misshapen animals or humans.

4: pollarded: where branches have been cut off

....
....

Source 7b: from 'Haunted Houses'
A house that people have thought it unsafe to pass after dark, and which has remained for years without a tenant, and which no tenant would occupy, even were he paid to do so.

....
....

11

SECTION A READING

Had a go ☐   Nearly there ☐   Nailed it! ☐

Fact, opinion and expert evidence

1 Draw lines to link the words in bold with the correct definition and example.

- something known to be true ——— **Fact** — Ed Sheeran is superior to all other musicians.
- the opinion of a person or group with special knowledge about a subject — **Opinion** — Malala Yousafzai was born on 12 July 1997.
- something a person believes that may or may not be true — **Expert evidence** — You should improve your diet and do more exercise to give you the best chance of living longer.

Read the short extract from **source 5a**, 'Googled your cough?', below. Then answer Questions 2 and 3.

> You may think I sound crazy but, actually, I just have a mild form of cyberchondria: a condition in which benign aches and pains are transformed into fatal diseases after a few minutes spent looking up symptoms on Google. It's a common ailment[1]: one in 20 Google searches are health-related and, according to a 2012 study, one in four British women have misdiagnosed themselves on the internet.

> Think about how the fact, opinion or expert evidence helps to support the writer's viewpoint or argument.

1: ailment: sickness

2 Write one sentence about the **writer's viewpoint** in the extract above. You can use your knowledge of facts, opinions and expert evidence to help you.

....

....

3 Complete the table below.

	Fact, opinion or expert evidence?	How does this support the writer's viewpoint?
… It's a common ailment		....
… I just have a mild form of cyberchondria		The writer, who has been published in a national newspaper says 'I just have a mild form of cyberchondria' and has quoted 'a 2012 study' in her article. By admitting her fears in a national newspaper and by providing expert evidence to support her, we believe the problem of 'cyberchondria' is a real one.
… one in 20 Google searches are health-related		....

> Remember that the person providing the expert evidence could be the writer of the text, as in this case!

Had a go ☐   Nearly there ☐   Nailed it! ☐

SECTION A READING

Explicit information and ideas

Read **lines 5 to 14** from **source 3**, 'The Yellow Wallpaper' on page 103, then look at the student answer to the exam-style question below. Think about what it is asking you to do, and how this student has stated the four possible answers.

> There is no need for a detailed explanation or analysis of language – you just simply need to identify the correct answers. First, identify the subject (in this case John). Then, use 'John … ' or 'He … ' at the beginning of every sentence.

Paper 1

Read again the first part of the source, **lines 1 to 3**.
1 List **four** things from this part of the text that we learn about John.   **(4 marks)**

(a) He's the narrator's husband.

(b) He laughs at his wife.

(c) He's a physician.

(d) He's very practical.

1 Now read **lines 1 to 9** from **source 4**, 'There Will Come Soft Rains', and answer the exam-style question below.

> In the living room the voice-clock sang, Tick-tock, seven o'clock, time to get up, time to get up, seven o'clock! as if it were afraid nobody would. The morning house lay empty. The clock ticked on, repeating and repeating its sounds into the emptiness. Seven-nine, breakfast time, seven-nine!
>
> In the kitchen the breakfast stove gave a hissing sigh and ejected from its warm interior eight pieces of perfectly browned toast, eight eggs sunnyside up, sixteen slices of bacon, two coffees, and two cool glasses of milk.
>
> 'Today is August 4, 2026,' said a second voice from the kitchen ceiling, 'in the city of Allendale, California.'

Paper 1

1 Read the first part of the source again, **lines 1 to 9**.
List **four** things from this part of the text that we discover about the house.   **(4 marks)**

(a) The house can make breakfast.

(b) The house ....

(c) ....

(d) ....

> You can also find **implicit** information for this question, but will not get extra marks for doing so. It is usually easier to find explicit information in the text, so stick to what is easiest to get the marks.
> You can use very short quotations from the text in you answer but do not copy whole, longer sentences.

2 Turn to the four sources on pages 101 to 104. For each source, see how many pieces of explicit information or ideas you can find in five minutes. A theme and line references have been given for each source to help guide your responses.

Record how many pieces of explicit information or ideas you found in each extract.

Rebecca ☐   The Kite Runner ☐
('Manderley', lines 32–36)   ('Hassan', lines 20–24)

'The Yellow Wallpaper' ☐   'There Will Come Soft Rains' ☐
('the house', lines 37–46)   (robot mice, lines 21–25)

SECTION A READING

Had a go ☐   Nearly there ☐   Nailed it! ☐

Implicit information and ideas

Finding implicit information and ideas is very important for **Section A: Reading**, **Paper 2**, **Question 2**. You will be asked to refer to details in **two** sources for this question.

Read the extracts from **source 5a**, 'Googled your cough?' by Arwa Mahdawi, and **source 5b**, 'The Boat to America' by Charles Dickens.

> **'Googled your cough? Is death now upon you?'**
> You may think I sound crazy but, actually, I just have a mild form of cyberchondria: a condition in which benign aches and pains are transformed into fatal diseases after a few minutes spent looking up symptoms on Google. It's a common ailment:[1] one in 20 Google searches are health-related and, according to a 2012 study, one in four British women have misdiagnosed themselves on the internet.

Mahdawi mocks the seriousness of 'cyberchondria' and uses hyperbole such as 'crazy' and 'fatal' to emphasise how the condition exaggerates symptoms.

1: ailment: sickness

> **'The Boat to America'**
> My own two hands, and feet likewise, being very cold, however, on this particular occasion, I crept below at midnight. It was not exactly comfortable below. It was decidedly close; and it was impossible to be unconscious of the presence of that extraordinary compound of strange smells, which is to be found nowhere but on board ship, and which is such a subtle perfume that it seems to enter at every pore of the skin, and whisper of the hold.
>
> Two passengers' wives (one of them my own) lay already in silent agonies on the sofa; and one lady's maid (my lady's) was a mere bundle on the floor, cursing her destiny. Everything sloped the wrong way: which in itself was an aggravation[10] scarcely to be borne.

Dickens shows genuine sympathy and concern for his wife and her...

....
....

10: aggravation: annoyance

Now look at this exam-style question relating to the extracts. **You don't need to answer it**. Instead, answer Questions 1 and 2 below.

Paper 2

> 2 Use details from both sources. Write a summary of the different ways Dickens and Mahdawi experience illness.
> **(8 marks)**

1 Annotate each extract with **two** pieces of implicit information/ideas you can find. The first two have been started for you.

2 Now write a paragraph summarising one of the differences between Mahdawi and Dickens. You could write about their differences in:

- how they find out about their symptoms (searching on the internet/using their senses)
- whether the symptoms are real or imagined
- whether or not they take their symptoms seriously.

> Remember, you will be looking at the whole of the source for this question, not just two short extracts. You can turn to source 5a on page 105 and source 5b on page 106 and have another go at the exam-style question.

....
....
....
....

14

Had a go ☐   Nearly there ☐   Nailed it! ☐

SECTION A READING

Inference

Read this extract from **source 2**, *The Kite Runner* by Khaled Hosseini, then answer Questions 1 and 2.

> December 2001
> I became what I am today at the age of twelve, on a frigid overcast day in the winter of 1975. I remember the precise moment, crouching behind a crumbling mud wall, peeking into the alley near the frozen creek. That was a long time ago, but it's wrong what they say about the past, I've learned, about how you can bury it. Because the past claws its way out. Looking back now, I realize I have been peeking into that deserted alley for the last twenty-six years.
> One day last summer, my friend Rahim Khan called from Pakistan. He asked me to come see him. Standing in the kitchen with the receiver to my ear, I knew it wasn't just Rahim Khan on the line. It was my past of unatoned sins. After I hung up, I went for a walk along Spreckels Lake on the northern edge of Golden Gate Park. The early-afternoon sun sparkled on the water where dozens of miniature boats sailed, propelled by a crisp breeze. Then I glanced up and saw a pair of kites, red with long blue tails, soaring in the sky. They danced high above the trees on the west end of the park, over the windmills, floating side by side like a pair of eyes looking down on San Francisco, the city I now call home. And suddenly Hassan's voice whispered in my head: For you, a thousand times over. Hassan the harelipped kite runner.
> I sat on a park bench near a willow tree. I thought about something Rahim Khan said just before he hung up, almost as an afterthought. There is a way to be good again.

1 Underline quotations from the text that support each of the four TRUE statements below. The first one has been done for you.

   A The narrator is an adult telling a story about his childhood.
   B The narrator can't forget what happened when he was a child.
   C The narrator emigrated to America.
   D The narrator has regrets about his life.

2 How does the writer use language to show that the narrator is troubled by his past?

....

....

....

Read this short extract, again from **source 2**, *The Kite Runner*, then answer Questions 3 and 4.

> Sometimes, up in those trees, I talked Hassan into firing walnuts with his slingshot at the neighbour's one-eyed German shepherd. Hassan never wanted to, but if I asked, really asked, he wouldn't deny me. Hassan never denied me anything. And he was deadly with his slingshot. Hassan's father, Ali, used to catch us and get mad, or as mad as someone as gentle as Ali could ever get.

3 Highlight or underline any phrases in the extract above that show us something about the narrator's relationship with Hassan.

4 What impression of Hassan do you get from this short extract? Include two points, and use a short quotation to support each point and back up your answer.

> Think about what is implied about a character by the actions of other characters in the scene, as well as the way the characters themselves behave.

(a) Hassan 'never denied' the narrator anything, which tells us that ....

....

(b) Hassan was 'deadly with his slingshot', suggesting ....

....

15

SECTION A READING Had a go ☐   Nearly there ☐   Nailed it! ☐

Point–Evidence–Explain

Read this short extract from **source 5b**, 'Googled your cough? Is death now upon you?', then answer Questions 1 to 5.

> Indeed, it's possible that, by now, you are starting to remember that your toe hurts, or you have a headache, or your leg is twitching. You may feel an urge to Google your symptoms. Hypochondriacs, please proceed with caution.

1   This point could be used to comment on the writer's use of language and its effect on the reader. Which piece of evidence below (A or B) most effectively supports this point? Circle your choice.

   Point: The writer uses a pattern of three to emphasise how looking up medical issues online can make you worry more about your health.

   Evidence A: 'You may feel an urge to Google your symptoms.'

   Evidence B: ' … your toe hurts, or you have a headache, or your leg is twitching.'

2   Explain why the evidence you have chosen is the most effective for supporting the above point.

   ....

   ....

3   Select effective evidence from the extract to support the point below. Then choose the most effective explanation from the options given. Circle your choice.

   Point: The writer uses direct address to make the reader think about their own health.

   Evidence: For example, she uses ....

   ....

   Explanation A: This direct address suggests to the reader that they might also be unwell.

   Explanation B: This direct address encourages the reader to feel anxious and question whether they are unwell. It also implies that the reader is becoming paranoid and has already started to consider checking their own symptoms on the internet.

4   Write one or two sentences, explaining which of the above you think is more effective and why.

   Explanation B is more effective because it is fully developed and more specific. This suggests that

   ....

   ....

   ....

> Point–Evidence–Explain, or P–E–E, is particularly useful if you are asked to comment on language and structure, or to evaluate or compare a text. Improve your P–E–E paragraphs by making sure you focus in on key words and explain the precise effect they have on the reader.

5   Choose a key word from the evidence you chose for your answer to Question 1. Explain why the writer used that word and what effect it has on the reader.

   ....

   ....

   ....

   ....

Had a go ☐   Nearly there ☐   Nailed it! ☐

SECTION A READING

Putting it into practice

Read the full extract from *Rebecca*, in **source 1** on page 101, then answer the exam-style questions below.

Guided

Paper ①

1 Read the first part of the source, **lines 1 to 5**, again and answer the exam-style question.

1 List four things you learn from this part of the text about Manderley.

(4 marks)

(a) ....
(b) ....
(c) ....
(d) ....

Guided

2 Now write one P–E–E paragraph of an answer to the exam-style question below.

> When you tackle this kind of question in the exam, remember to:
> - spend about 10 minutes on your answer
> - identify the main focus of the question
> - read the text carefully and annotate it with your ideas
> - only use the lines of the extract referred to in the question
> - comment on how the writer uses language and structure and what the effects are on the reader.

Paper ①

2 Look in detail at **lines 8 to 40** of the source.
How does the writer use language here to create an atmosphere around Manderley?
You could include the writer's choice of:
- words and phrases
- language features and techniques
- sentence forms.

(8 marks)

....
....
....
....
....
....
....
....
....
....
....

> **Remember:** You are only being asked to write part of an answer on this page. In the exam, where you will write a full answer, you will have more space for your answer.

Had a go ☐   Nearly there ☐   Nailed it! ☐

Putting it into practice

 Read the full extract from 'Haunted Houses' in **source 7b** on page 110. Then write three P–E–E paragraphs of an answer to the exam-style question below.

> This kind of question needs you to analyse language. Make sure that you:
> - spend about 12 minutes on your answer
> - identify the main focus of the question
> - read the text carefully and annotate it with your ideas
> - write P–E–E paragraphs to explain how the writer uses specific language techniques, words or phrases to create an effect.

Paper 2

3   You now need to refer **only** to **source 7b**. How does the writer use language to interest the reader in haunted houses? **(12 marks)**

....
....
....
....
....
....
....
....
....
....
....
....
....
....
....
....
....
....
....
....
....
....

> **Remember:** You are only being asked to write part of an answer on this page. In the exam, where you will write a full answer, you will have more space for your writing.

Had a go ☐   Nearly there ☐   Nailed it! ☐

SECTION A READING

Word classes

Read this short extract from **source 7a**, 'Creating ghost stories', then answer Questions 1 and 2.

Most of the Brothers Grimm tales are *positively* frightening. It is embedded deep within our psyche, that feeling of something outside of our control, lingering in a particular spot. Would you not expect someone or something to shadow you into that uncertain grey distance… some water sprite cling to your boots or leggings to drag you into that damp uncertainty?

1 Underline and label as many examples of each of the following word classes as you can. Two have been done for you:
- noun
- verb
- adverb
- adjective.

> Forgotten your word classes? Don't worry, just remember:
> **noun:** is the name of a thing, person, place or idea (e.g. 'pen', 'builder', 'hospital' or 'happiness')
> **verb:** usually describes an action (physical or mental) such as 'shouting', 'ran', 'believe', 'considering'
> **adverb:** gives more information about the verb (e.g. 'The boy ran *quickly*')
> **adjective:** describes a noun (e.g. 'The *large* dog splashed in the *filthy* puddle').
> Adjectives can be **compound** (joined with a hyphen, e.g. 'multi-million')
> Remember that adjectives can become **comparatives** (e.g. 'noisier', 'more insolent') and **superlatives** (e.g. 'noisiest', 'most insolent').

Now read this short extract from **source 4**, 'There Will Come Soft Rains', then answer Question 3.

Outside, the garage chimed and lifted its door to reveal the waiting car. After a long wait the door swung down again.

At eight-thirty the eggs were shrivelled and the toast was like stone. An aluminium wedge scraped them down a metal throat which digested and flushed them away to the distant sea. The dirty dishes were dropped into a hot washer and emerged twinkling dry.

2 The writer uses adjectives to describe the machines and breakfast things. What effect do these have on the reader?

The adjectives build up a picture in the reader's mind of the transformation of the 'dirty' dishes ....

....

The machine strikes the reader as ....

....

Guided

3 In this extract, the writer uses action verbs to explain the routine of the computer-controlled house. Identify two examples of action verbs and explain their effects on the reader.

(a) ....

....

....

(b) ....

....

....

> An action verb is a verb that expresses physical or mental action.

| SECTION A READING | Had a go ☐   Nearly there ☐   Nailed it! ☐ |

Connotations

Read this short extract from **source 6a**, 'Women aren't "better" at housework', then answer Question 1.

> As (boring) as housework can be – as a literal chore or as a political issue – we can't continue to treat it as ancillary³ to the larger (fight) for women's (equality). What happens in our homes matters, as does women's time and how they spend it. It's core to feminism⁴.

3: ancillary: additional   **4: feminism**: belief in equal rights for women

1 (a) Complete the table by writing the connotations suggested by the circled words. One has been done for you.

boring	dull, unimportant
fight	
equality	

> Words can have different meanings depending on their context – what comes before and after them in a text. Thinking about the context of a word will help you to understand its connotations.

(b) Using your completed table, how do the connotations associated with the circled words contribute to the extract's overall message?

....

....

Now read this short extract from **source 3**, 'The Yellow Wallpaper', then answer Question 2.

> The colour is repellent, almost revolting; a smouldering⁷ unclean yellow, strangely faded by the slow-turning sunlight.
> It is a dull yet lurid orange in some places, a sickly sulphur tint in others.

7: smouldering: burn slowly, with smoke but no fire

2 Choose two words or phrases the writer uses to describe the wallpaper. Write a brief sentence to explain the literal meaning. Then write the connotations.

(a) smouldering unclean ....

Literal meaning	Smouldering means burning slowly but with no flame. Unclean means dirty.
Connotations	The word 'smouldering' gives the impression that the paper is alive or festering in some way, almost as if it is moving. Describing the colour yellow as 'unclean' suggests ....

(b) ....

Literal meaning	....
Connotations	....

> Remember to look at the context of the extract above. How do you think the narrator feels about her surroundings?

Had a go ☐ Nearly there ☐ Nailed it! ☐

SECTION A READING

Figurative language

Read this short extract from **source 4**, 'There Will Come Soft Rains', then answer Question 1.

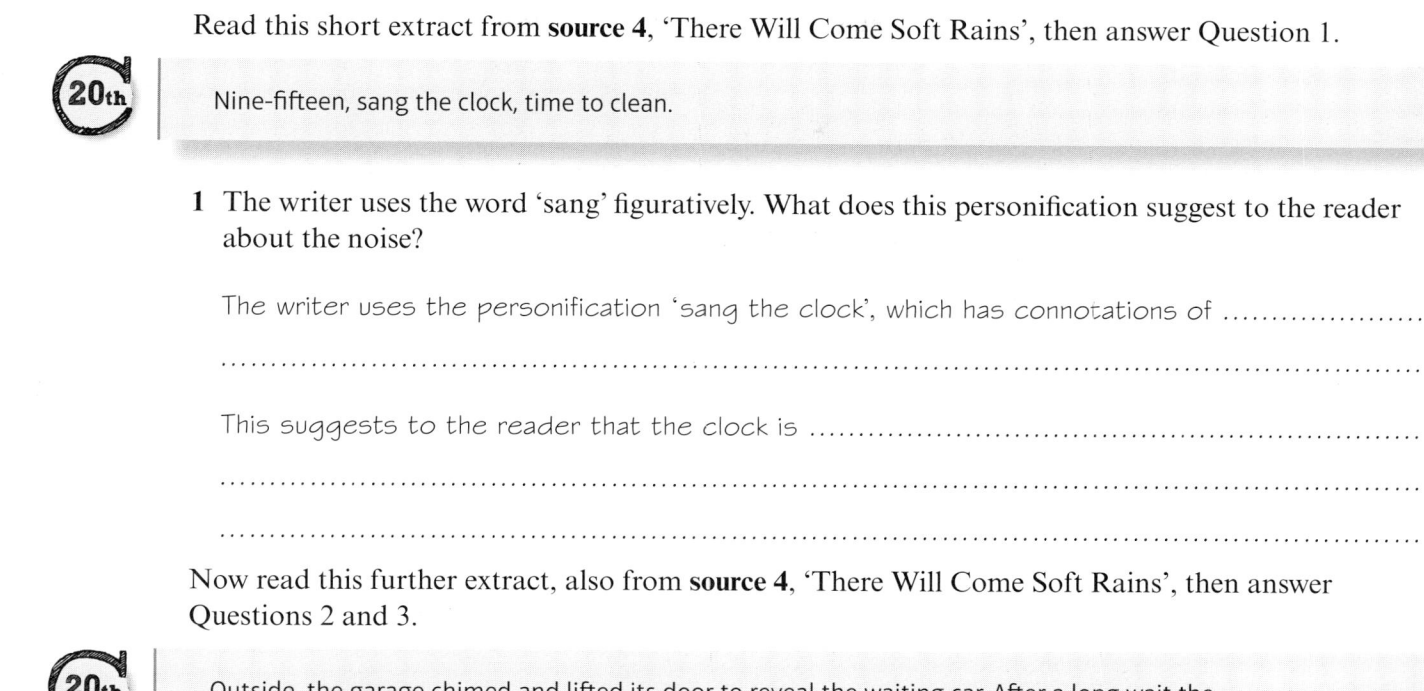

> Nine-fifteen, sang the clock, time to clean.

1 The writer uses the word 'sang' figuratively. What does this personification suggest to the reader about the noise?

The writer uses the personification 'sang the clock', which has connotations of ....

....

This suggests to the reader that the clock is ....

....

....

Now read this further extract, also from **source 4**, 'There Will Come Soft Rains', then answer Questions 2 and 3.

> Outside, the garage chimed and lifted its door to reveal the waiting car. After a long wait the door swung down again.
> At eight-thirty the eggs were shrivelled and the toast was like stone. An aluminium wedge scraped them down a metal throat which digested and flushed them away to the distant sea. The dirty dishes were dropped into a hot washer and emerged twinkling dry.

2 The writer uses the simile 'the toast was like stone'. What does this suggest about the toast?

How does it feel? ....

How appetising is it? ....

How long has it been there? ....

Why is it still there? ....

> Don't just identify and name a figurative device used in a text. Remember to comment on the effect the device has on the reader.

3 Identify a metaphor the writer has used in the extract above. (**Hint: look closely at the second section.**) Write a P–E–E paragraph explaining why the writer has used it and its effect on the reader.

> Remember that a metaphor uses comparison to say one thing **is** something else, not just **like** something else.

The writer continues to make the house sound alive. ....

....

....

....

....

....

Creation of character

Read this short extract from 'The Yellow Wallpaper', then answer Question 1.

> I get <u>unreasonably angry</u> with John sometimes. I'm sure I never used to be <u>so sensitive</u>. I think it is due to this nervous condition.
>
> But John says if I feel so, I shall neglect proper self-control; so I take pains to control myself – before him, at least, and that makes me very tired.
>
> <u>I don't like our room a bit</u>. I wanted one downstairs that opened on the piazza⁴ and had roses all over the window, and such pretty old-fashioned chintz⁵ hangings! but John would not hear of it.
>
> He said there was only one window and not room for two beds, and no near room for him if he took another.
>
> He is very careful and loving, and hardly lets me stir without special direction.
>
> I have a schedule prescription for each hour in the day; <u>he takes all care from me</u>, and so I feel basely ungrateful not to value it more.
>
> He said we came here solely on my account, that I was to have perfect rest and all the air I could get. 'Your exercise depends on your strength, my dear,' said he, 'and your food somewhat on your appetite; but air you can absorb all the time.' So we took the nursery at the top of the house.

4: piazza: a square patio space   **5: chintz**: a printed, patterned fabric

1 How do the narrator's thoughts in the extract above build up an idea of her character? Annotate the text, using the underlined quotations to help you.

> Character can be created through dialogue, description or action.

Turn to the full extract from 'The Yellow Wallpaper' in **source 3** on page 103. Read **lines 15 to 30**, focusing on the narrator's character, then answer Question 2.

2 Write a P–E–E paragraph about how the writer creates an impression of the narrator's character. Use the table to help you plan:

Quotation for evidence	
Technique being explored	
Explanation 1	
Explanation 2	

The writer shows that the narrator is uncomfortable in her surroundings. ....

....

....

....

....

....

....

....

....

....

....

Had a go ☐   Nearly there ☐   Nailed it! ☐

SECTION A READING

Creating atmosphere

Read this short extract from **source 3**, 'The Yellow Wallpaper', then answer Questions 1 to 3.

> It is a big, <u>airy</u> room, the whole floor nearly, with windows that look all ways, and air and sunshine galore. It was nursery first and then playroom and gymnasium, I should judge; for the windows are barred for little children, and there are rings and things in the walls.
>
> The paint and paper (look) as if a boys' school had used it. It is stripped off – the paper – in great patches all around the head of my bed, about as far as I can reach, and in a great place on the other side of the room low down. I never saw a worse paper in my life.
>
> One of those <u>sprawling</u> flamboyant[6] patterns committing every artistic sin.
>
> It is dull enough to (confuse) the eye in following, pronounced enough to constantly irritate and provoke study, and when you follow the lame uncertain curves for a little distance they suddenly commit suicide – plunge off at outrageous angles, (destroy) themselves in unheard of contradictions.
>
> The colour is <u>repellent</u>, almost revolting; a <u>smouldering</u>[7] <u>unclean</u> yellow, strangely faded by the slow-turning sunlight.

6: flamboyant: attracting attention because of its over-the-top colour and brightness
7: smouldering: burn slowly, with smoke but no fire

1 Connotations help to create atmosphere. What are the connotations of the following words and phrases from the extract above?

Quotation	Literal (explicit) meaning	Connotation (implicit meaning)
'the windows are barred'	There are bars on the window	This sounds like a prison, somewhere to keep the narrator trapped.
'repellent'		
'smouldering'		

2 (a) Circle all the action verbs and underline the adjectives in the extract that help to create atmosphere. Some have been done for you.

   (b) How do the action verbs and adjectives contribute to the atmosphere of the room?

   ....

   ....

3 In the answer extracts below, students have commented on the atmosphere in the first half of the extract above from 'The Yellow Wallpaper'. They have used their answers to Question 1 to plan their writing. Write an improved version of the student answers that fully explains the connotations of individual words and uses a P–E–E structure.

   A

   > A tense atmosphere is created by the writer's description 'the windows are barred' which makes it sound like a prison.

   ....
   ....

   B

   > The writer creates a tense atmosphere in the adjective 'barred' which has connotations of prison, contrasting with the nursery the narrator describes.
   > The verb 'smouldering' also has a sense of threat.

   ....
   ....
   ....
   ....

SECTION A READING

Had a go ☐ Nearly there ☐ Nailed it! ☐

Narrative voice

> Narrative voice is the 'voice' a writer of fiction chooses to tell the story. A writer can choose a narrative voice to create a particular point of view. The narrative voice is **not** the voice of the writer but a created character.

Read extracts A and B below and then answer questions Questions 1 and 2.

Extract A: from 'There Will Come Soft Rains'
In the kitchen the breakfast stove gave a hissing sigh and ejected from its warm interior eight pieces of perfectly browned toast, eight eggs sunnyside up, sixteen slices of bacon, two coffees, and two cool glasses of milk.

'Today is August 4, 2026' said a second voice from the kitchen ceiling, 'in the city of Allendale, California.' It repeated the date three times for memory's sake. 'Today is Mr. Featherstone's birthday. Today is the anniversary of Tilita's marriage. Insurance is payable, as are the water, gas, and light bills.'

Extract B: from *Rebecca*
Last night I dreamt I went to Manderley again. It seemed to me I stood by the iron gate leading to the drive, and for a while I could not enter, for the way was barred to me. There was a padlock and chain upon the gate. I called in my dream to the lodge-keeper, and had no answer, and peering closer through the rusted spokes of the gate I saw that the lodge was uninhabited.

1 Read the statements below and tick the boxes to show which extract they refer to. One has been done for you.

	Extract A	Extract B
This extract is written in the first person.	☐	✓
This extract has an omniscient, third person narrator.	☐	☐
The use of narrative voice in this extract reveals the narrator's own experiences.	☐	☐

2 Reread Extract B. Write one clear paragraph commenting on how the writer's use of narrative voice influences the reader's feelings towards the narrator.

The writer's use of first person narration ....

Had a go ☐   Nearly there ☐   Nailed it! ☐

SECTION A READING

Putting it into practice

 Read the full extract from *The Kite Runner*, in **source 2** on page 102, then answer the exam-style question below.

Paper ①

2 Look in detail at this extract from lines 25 to 36 of the source.
How does the writer use language here to present the characters' personalities and appearances?
You could include the writer's choice of:
- words and phrases
- language features and techniques
- sentence forms (e.g. complex, simple, compound). **(8 marks)**

When you tackle this type of question in the exam, remember to:
- spend around 10 minutes on your answer
- read the question carefully and highlight the main focus
- read the source text thoroughly, annotating as you read
- only use the lines of the text referred to in the question
- identify and name the language used and comment on its effects
- support all your points with clear evidence and a clear explanation by using a P–E–E structure in your paragraphs.

In the exam you should try and use the technical names for language devices as well as explaining the effect they create. Here you need to comment on how the writer uses language – skills you have covered on pages 19 to 24.

Remember to try to refer to specific language techniques in the exam, for example: metaphor, imagery, verb, simile, connotation.

....
....
....
....
....
....
....
....
....
....
....
....
....
....
....
....
....

Remember: You have more space than this to answer your question in the exam. Use your own paper to finish your answer to the question above.

SECTION A READING

Had a go ☐   Nearly there ☐   Nailed it! ☐

Putting it into practice

Read the full extract from 'Haunted Houses', in **source 7b** on page 110, then answer the exam-style question below.

Paper ②

3 You now need to refer **only** to **source 7b**.
   How does the narrator use language to suggest the unpleasant nature of the house? **(12 marks)**

> When you tackle this type of question in the exam, remember to:
> - spend around 12 minutes on your answer
> - read the question carefully and highlight the main focus
> - read the source text thoroughly, annotating as you read
> - only use the lines of the text referred to in the question
> - identify the language and structural devices used and comment on their effects
> - support all your points with clear evidence and a clear explanation by using a P–E–E structure in your paragraphs.

> **Remember:** You are only being asked to write part of an answer on this page. In the exam, where you will write a full answer, you will have more space for your writing.

Had a go ☐   Nearly there ☐   Nailed it! ☐

SECTION A READING

Rhetorical devices 1

Read this short extract from **source 7b**, 'Haunted Houses', then answer the questions below.

> Who has not either seen or heard of some house, shut up and uninhabitable, fallen into decay, and looking dusty and dreary, from which, at midnight, strange sounds have been heard to issue the rattling of chains, and the groaning of perturbed[1] spirits?

1: perturbed: anxious or unsettled

1 Find one example of alliteration in the extract above.

   ....

   > Writers use rhetorical devices to emphasise their points or to manipulate the reader's response.

2 The extract above is an example of a rhetorical question. How does this question encourage the reader to engage with the text as a whole?

   It encourages readers to look out for warning signs ....

   ....

   ....

   ....

3 Reread the extract above and comment on how the writer uses rhetorical devices to influence the reader's opinion of haunted houses.

   You should identify at least two different rhetorical devices, suggest why the writer has used them and explain the intended effect on the reader. Some devices are:
   - pattern of three
   - lists
   - alliteration
   - emotive language
   - rhetorical questions.

   The answer has been started for you.

   > Remember to clearly explain the effect the device has on the reader. Think about how the device makes the reader feel.

   The writer lists some of the qualities associated with the stereotypical haunted house. The reader is encouraged to imagine a house that is 'uninhabitable, fallen into decay, and looking dusty and dreary'. This series of negative images, all included within a single extended sentence, potentially overwhelms the reader by giving the opening of the text a notably dark tone. The writer also uses ....

   ....

   ....

   ....

   ....

   ....

Rhetorical devices 2

Read this short extract from **source 6a**, 'Women aren't "better" at housework' by Jessica Valenti, then answer Question 1.

> So it's not just physical labour – like vacuuming or scrubbing toilets – that's running us down, it's the day-to-day mental work. We're not just shopping, we're making the grocery lists. We're not just cleaning, we're figuring out what's dirty.

1 The writer is frustrated by the amount of time women spend on housework. How does the repetition of 'we're' help to show her attitude of frustration?

   The writer's use of repetition implies that household chores are something that women ....

   ....

   ....

Now read the next paragraph from 'Women aren't "better" at housework'. Then answer Questions 2 and 3.

> Thinking about doing chores may not *seem* like a lot of work – but consider what an incredible privilege it is to have your mind free of multitasking. <u>Men who don't have to think about which chores have to be done</u> and who is going to do them have the luxury of headspace to think more about work, hobbies or *any damn thing they want*. Women, meanwhile, are trying to figure out if the kids need any more juice boxes that week. (Speaking of kids, the latest numbers don't even take child care into account, a huge – albeit[2] cute – time suck for women.)

2: albeit: even though

2 The underlined section in the extract above provides a contrast (an opposing or different idea) to the jobs done by women in the first extract on this page. Write one or two sentences explaining how this use of contrast helps to demonstrate the writer's frustrated attitude about women and housework.

   ....

   ....

   ....

> If you know it, use the technical name for the device in your answer. If you don't know the technical name, you should still comment on the language and its effect.

3 Identify **one metaphor** and **one example of colloquial language** used in the second extract above. Write one or two sentences commenting on why the writer has used each device and the effect each one has on the reader. An example commenting on direct address has been done for you.

Device	Example	Effect and purpose
Direct address	'consider what an incredible privilege'	Asks the reader to think; provokes their own opinion. Creates relationship between writer and reader.
Metaphor		
Colloquial language		

Had a go ☐   Nearly there ☐   Nailed it! ☐

SECTION A READING

Whole text structure: fiction

Read the full extract from 'There Will Come Soft Rains', in **source 4** on page 104. Now focus on these lines from the source.

> <u>At eight-thirty the eggs were shrivelled and the toast was like stone.</u> An aluminium wedge scraped them down a metal throat which digested and flushed them away to the distant sea. The dirty dishes were dropped into a hot washer and emerged twinkling dry.
>
> Nine-fifteen, sang the clock, time to clean. Out of warrens in the wall, tiny robot mice darted. The rooms were acrawl with the small cleaning animals, all rubber and metal. They thudded against chairs, whirling their moustached runners, kneading the rug nap, sucking gently at hidden dust. <u>Then, like mysterious invaders, they popped into their burrows.</u> Their pink electric eyes faded. The house was clean.
>
> Ten o'clock. The sun came out from behind the rain. The house stood alone in a city of rubble and ashes. This was the one house left standing. At night the ruined city gave of a radioactive glow which could be seen for miles.

Read Question 1 and the example answer, then answer the questions that follow.

1 How does the writer use time to structure their ideas?

Bradbury starts his story at 'eight-thirty' when breakfast is being cleared, implying that the family living there should have left for work but if they have, they have done without eating the breakfast prepared. By using 'nine-fifteen' and 'ten o'clock' Bradbury shows time passing quickly, and the house cleaning itself in a pre-programmed routine — but without the people in the house this becomes eerie and strange.

2 How do the sentences underlined above foreshadow the dramatic revelation that follows later in the source?

The fact that nobody eats the breakfast suggests ....

....

The robotic 'invaders' highlights the lack of ....

....

Now focus on what happens next in the source, before answering Question 3.

> Ten-fifteen. The garden sprinklers whirled up in golden founts, filling the soft morning air with scatterings of brightness. The water pelted windowpanes, running down the charred west side where the house had been burned evenly free of its white paint. The entire west face of the house was black, save for five places. Here the silhouette in paint of a man mowing a lawn. Here, as in a photograph, a woman bent to pick flowers. Still farther over, their images burned on wood in one titanic instant, a small boy, hands flung into the air; higher up, the image of thrown ball, and opposite him a girl, hand raised to catch a ball which never came down. The five spots of paint – the man, the woman, the children, the ball – remained. The rest was a thin charcoaled layer. The gentle sprinkler rain filled the garden with falling light.

3 What is the effect of this structure on the reader?

The description of the family's burned shadows ....

....

The final sentence 'filled the garden with falling light' creates a mood of ....

....

> Remember that writers of fiction use a variety of narrative structures for effect. These include foreshadowing, use of closely described detail or action, repetition and dialogue.

SECTION A READING

Had a go ☐   Nearly there ☐   Nailed it! ☐

Whole text structure: non-fiction

Read this short extract from **source 7a**, an online article by Robert Hallmann that was originally published on The History Press website, then answer Question 1. The extract provides the article's heading and opening paragraph.

Creating ghost stories

Essex, in spite of its friendly and prosperous present, has an ancient history of Roman invaders and Saxon immigrants, Pagan[1] groves and Christian conversions, Viking raiders, Norman conquerors, Civil War battles and sieges, witches, witch-hunts and witch trials, smugglers on its convoluting coast and highwaymen in its extensive forests, not forgetting more recently Zeppelin disasters and bombing raids.

1: Pagan: relating to an ancient religious community based on the worship of nature

1 Suggest how the heading and opening paragraph introduce the subject of the article and convey the writer's viewpoint to the reader.

The headline and opening paragraph contrast the 'friendly and prosperous' present with a long list of violent events from the past. This is an effective way to start an article entitled 'creating ghost stories' as it shows ....

....

....

2 Consider the following ways in which writers can end their writing in order to leave a lasting impression:

- vivid images
- calls to action
- a rhetorical question
- warnings
- advice
- summary of main points

(a) Based on the start of the article, circle the one you think would be most suitable for Robert Hallmann to use at the end of the article.

(b) What evidence from the heading or the opening led you to make your choice?

....

....

Now read the following extract, the concluding sentences to Hallmann's article. Then answer Question 2.

Today, with the aid of Photoshop, we can add some extra frisson[5] to images that may add a touch of danger or mystery to set the imagination racing. Set in a time research has made familiar, mix scene and story into the cauldron, that's an interesting formula to me.

> When you answer questions about structure it's important to look at the way that ideas and tones change throughout the extract and how these can contribute to the text's overall meaning.

5: frisson: excitement or fear

3 Consider both of the extracts above and their position within the article as a whole. Explain how the writer uses structure for effect. You should link your ideas to the writer's point of view and intended purpose and audience. The answer has been started for you.

The opening to the article introduces the topic of ghost stories in an engaging way through the juxtaposition of the 'friendly' present with the violence of the past. Hallmann further engages the reader by showing, from the first sentence, how the past can be embellished for dramatic effect. ....

....

....

....

Had a go ☐   Nearly there ☐   Nailed it! ☐

SECTION A READING

Identifying sentence types

1 Look at the table. Draw lines to match the sentences A–D to the correct sentence type.

A	Every nerve was jangling.	minor sentence
B	Although I knew what was coming, I couldn't work out how to stop it.	multi-clause sentence (coordinate)
C	I opened the door and my feet froze to the floor.	multi-clause sentence (subordinate)
D	Complete melt-down.	single-clause sentence

Now read this short extract from **source 5a**, 'Googled your cough?', then answer Question 2.

> At 11am I had a strange pain in my toe. By 11.05 I was convinced it was a brain tumour. By 11.15 I'd realised that, actually, my shoes were probably to blame, but by that time I'd already decided on the music that should be played at my funeral.
>
> You may think I sound crazy but, actually, I just have a mild form of cyberchondria: a condition in which benign aches and pains are transformed into fatal diseases after a few minutes spent looking up symptoms on Google. It's a common ailment[1]: one in 20 Google searches are health-related and, according to a 2012 study, one in four British women have misdiagnosed themselves on the internet.

1: ailment: sickness

2 (a) In the extract above, find one example of each kind of sentence and write it below:

Single-clause ....

....

Multi-clause (subordinate) ....

....

Multi-clause (coordinate) ....

....

> SINGLE-CLAUSE sentences are made up of just **one clause, or section**, and provide **one piece of information** about an event or action. They contain a **subject** and one **verb**.
> MULTI-CLAUSE sentences are made up of **more than one clause**. They contain **two or more verbs**.
> SUBORDINATE clauses do not make sense on their own. They are **dependent** on the main clause.
> COORDINATE clauses are an **equal pair**, where neither clause is dependent on the other. Each clause contains a verb.
> MINOR SENTENCES are grammatically incomplete because they **do not contain a verb**.

(b) Look at the different example sentences above. Choose one and make some notes about the effect this sentence type has on the reader.

....
....
....
....
....
....

SECTION A READING

Had a go ☐   Nearly there ☐   Nailed it! ☐

Commenting on sentences

Read this short extract from **source 7a**, 'Creating ghost stories', then answer Questions 1 and 2.

> There has been so much personal terror, so much anguish, so much blood soaked into Essex soil, that it is perhaps not surprising that there are so many tales of hauntings, of supernatural sightings and unexplainable experiences. Can you imagine Valkyries[2] or witches riding in such a sky, on such a day?
>
> Like a simmering undercurrent this past lingers on into the present. A writer just has to tap into that flow of evidence and it can read like stories. The lore and traditions are as colourful as any county's. At least that is how I perceive the tales that I hope to have added to its treasury. A tale may be new, but if it is set in a particular time and place, it – or something rather similar – may well have happened.

2: Valkyries: Norse female warriors

Guided

1 The source starts with one long sentence followed by a rhetorical question. What is the effect of this on the reader?

....

....

2 The last sentence separates a subordinate clause in the middle of the sentence by using dashes: '– or something rather similar –'. What is the effect?

By presenting the subordinate clause in this way, the writer focuses attention on it. This has

the effect of diverting attention ....

Now read this short extract from **source 3**, 'The Yellow Wallpaper', then answer Question 3.

> I did write for a while in spite of them; but it DOES exhaust me a good deal – having to be so sly about it, or else meet with heavy opposition.
>
> I sometimes fancy that in my condition if I had less opposition and more society and stimulus[3] – but John says the very worst thing I can do is to think about my condition, and I confess it always makes me feel bad.
>
> So I will let it alone and talk about the house.

3: stimulus: something that creates activity or energy

3 In this source, the writer uses a variety of sentence types to create a sense of tension. Explain how the sentence structures create tension.

By starting with several long sentences with subordinate clauses, the narrator sounds ....

....

The final short sentence creates a contrasting impression of ....

....

The use of capital letters midway through a sentence ....

....

....

....

....

Had a go ☐ **Nearly there** ☐ **Nailed it!** ☐

SECTION A
READING

Putting it into practice

Read the full extract from 'The Yellow Wallpaper', in **source 3** on page 103, then answer the exam-style question below.

Paper ①

3   You now need to think about the whole of the source.
    How has the writer structured the text to interest you as a reader?
    You could write about:
    - what the writer focuses your attention on at the beginning
    - how and why the writer changes this focus as the extract develops
    - any other structural features that interest you.

    (8 marks)

> When you tackle this type of question in the exam, remember to:
> - spend around 8 minutes on your answer
> - read the question carefully and highlight the main focus
> - read the source text thoroughly, annotating as you read
> - refer to the whole of the source
> - identify the structural devices used and comment on their effects.

....

> **Remember:** You have more space than this to answer your question in the exam. Use your own paper to finish your answer to the question above.

Had a go ☐ **Nearly there** ☐ **Nailed it!** ☐

Putting it into practice

Read the full extract from 'Creating ghost stories', in **source 7a** on page 109, then answer the exam-style question below.

Paper ②

3 You now need to refer only to this source.
   How does the writer use language to persuade the reader of the power of imagination?

(12 marks)

> When you tackle this type of question in the exam, remember to:
> - spend around 12 minutes on your answer
> - read the question carefully and highlight the main focus
> - read the source text thoroughly, annotating as you read
> - identify the language and structural devices used and comment on their effects.

> **Remember**: You have more space than this to answer your question in the exam. Use your own paper to finish your answer to the question above.

Had a go ☐   Nearly there ☐   Nailed it! ☐

SECTION A READING

Evaluating a fiction text 1

Question 4 in **Paper 1, Section A: Reading** asks you to evaluate a text critically. This means you will need to make a judgement as a reader about how successful you think a particular aspect of the text is, and explain your thinking.

> To 'evaluate' means to look at different opinions and arguments, then come to a conclusion about your own interpretation.

Read the full extract from **source 2**, *The Kite Runner*, on page 102. Then read the exam-style question below. **You do not need to answer this question**. Then answer Questions 1 and 2.

> **4** Focus this part of your answer on the final section of the source, from line 20 to the end.
> A student, having read this section of the text said: 'In these lines, the writer creates a sense that the narrator's relationship with Hassan is unequal.'
> To what extent do you agree with this view?
> In your response, you could:
> - write about your own impressions of extract's tone
> - evaluate how the writer has created these impressions
> - support your opinions with quotations from the text.
>
> **(20 marks)**

1 Plan a response to the exam-style question using the following table to organise your thoughts. You should try to complete the plan in 2–3 minutes.

Think about:	Quick notes
(a) the purpose of the text – what impact does the writer intend to have on the reader?	
(b) how successful is the writer in achieving a particular effect?	
(c) how successful is the writer in drawing you into the text?	
(d) alternative interpretations of the text – how might other readers respond?	

> You can use quotations to back up your points but you don't need to analyse the language or structure in detail.

> When you answer an evaluation question you need to compare ideas from different parts of the source.

Guided **2** Reread the exam-style question and the extract from *The Kite Runner*. Write one or two compelling sentences for each of the reader responses below. Include evidence from the text to support each response.

I completely agree with this view ...

....

....

I partly agree with this view ...

....

....

I wholly disagree with this view ...

....

....

35

SECTION A READING

Had a go ☐   Nearly there ☐   Nailed it! ☐

Evaluating a fiction text 2

> Remember that 'evaluate' means to assess, or to weigh up. When evaluating a fiction text you need to justify your ideas using short, relevant quotations.

Read the full extract from *Rebecca*, in **source 1** on page 101, then read the exam-style question below. **You don't need to answer it**. Instead, answer Questions 1 and 2 below.

Paper 1

4   Focus this part of your answer on the first half of the source, from **lines 1 to 52**.
    A student, having read this section of the text, said: 'The writer has presented the narrator as uncertain, haunted by her past and her dreams.'
    To what extent do you agree?
    In your response, you could:
    - write about your own impressions of the narrator
    - evaluate how the writer has created these impressions
    - support your opinions with quotations from the text.

    (20 marks)

1   Underline and annotate the extract from *Rebecca* below as if you were preparing to answer the exam question. You should look for evidence that both supports and challenges the student's opinion.

> On and on, now east now west, wound the poor thread that once had been our drive. Sometimes I thought it lost, but it appeared again, beneath a fallen tree perhaps, or struggling on the other side of a muddied ditch created by the winter rains. I had not thought the way so long. Surely the miles had multiplied, even as the trees had done, and this path led but to a labyrinth⁵, some choked wilderness, and not to the house at all. I came upon it suddenly; the approach masked by the unnatural growth of a vast shrub that spread in all directions, and I stood, my heart thumping in my breast, the strange prick of tears behind my eyes.

5: labyrinth: maze

> Look for words and phrases that characterise the narrator.

2   Using your annotations from Question 1, write the first paragraph of your answer to the exam-style question.

> You should include both sides of the argument in your response so it is important to find evidence for each side in the text. Remember to clearly state your opinion and suggest how the writer's use of specific language techniques support it.

The writer effectively encourages the reader to see the narrator as both uncertain ....

....

....

However ....

....

....

> **Remember:** You are only being asked to write part of an answer on this page. In the exam, you will be given more space to write a full answer.

Had a go ☐   Nearly there ☐   Nailed it! ☐

SECTION A READING

Using evidence to evaluate

When using evidence in the evaluation question, think about how to use quotations effectively to **support** or **challenge** the statement in the question. Sometimes, the same statement can be interpreted in different ways so that you can support **and** challenge it.

Study the student annotations below. Students have been asked whether or not they agree that the narrator in 'The Yellow Wallpaper' appears deceitful. The annotations show that the student both agrees and disagrees with the question.

> I get unreasonably angry with John sometimes. I'm sure I never used to be so sensitive. I think it is due to this nervous condition.
>
> But John says if I feel so, I shall neglect proper self-control; so I take pains to control myself – before him, at least, and that makes me very tired.
>
> I don't like our room a bit. I wanted one downstairs that opened on the piazza⁴ and had roses all over the window, and such pretty old-fashioned chintz⁵ hangings! but John would not hear of it.

4: piazza: a square patio space
5: chintz: a printed, patterned fabric

This quotation could support the idea that the narrator is lying. The hesitation shown by the dash, and the modification 'at least' both suggest that she is not telling the complete truth, and that she is deliberately trying to present herself differently in front of her husband, which takes a lot of effort for her.

The narrator seems unable to control herself entirely. Her adjectival phrase 'I'm sure' shows that she is confused by her condition, compared with how she used to be. The adverb suggests that she knows she is behaving in a way that is inappropriate, but it seems out of her control and due to her 'nervous condition'.

1 Re-read the second half of 'The Yellow Wallpaper' in **source 3** on page 103, from **line 53 to the end**. Provide evidence to support and challenge the following statement: 'The narrator is being imprisoned by her husband.' Find a quotation and annotate it in the same way as the example. One example has been chosen for you.

   Quotation: 'He is very careful and loving, and hardly lets me stir without special direction.'

   Support: That he won't let her 'stir without special direction' shows he is ....
   ....

   Challenge: The adjectives 'careful and loving' show her husband is ....
   ....
   ....

   Quotation: ....
   Support: ....
   ....
   Challenge: ....
   ....

> Remember to put the quotation in quotation marks. When using quotations, remember that:
> - short quotations are most effective
> - you must use quotations rather than paraphrasing when explaining the effects of language
> - all quotations must be in quotation marks and copied correctly from the text.

SECTION A READING

Had a go ☐   Nearly there ☐   Nailed it! ☐

Putting it into practice

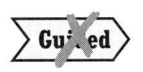

Guided

Read the full extract from 'There Will Come Soft Rains', in **source 4** on page 104, then answer the exam-style question below.

Paper 1

> **4** Focus this part of your answer on the second half of the source, from line 29 to the end.
> A student, having read this section of the text, said: 'The writer has created a shocking revelation, suggesting that the destruction was on a massive scale.'
> To what extent do you agree?
> In your response, you could:
> - write about your own impressions of the ending
> - evaluate how the writer has created these impressions
> - support your opinions with quotations from the text.
>
> **(20 marks)**

> When you tackle this type of question in the exam, remember to:
> - spend around 20 minutes on your answer
> - read the question carefully and highlight the main focus
> - read the source text thoroughly, annotating as you read
> - only use the lines of the text referred to in the question
> - use inference and evidence from the text to explain your ideas and assess the effect of the text.

> **Remember:** You have more space than this to answer your question in the exam. Use your own paper to finish your answer to the question above.

Had a go ☐ Nearly there ☐ Nailed it! ☐

SECTION A READING

Writing about two texts

In **Paper 2**, **Section A: Reading**, Questions 2 and 4 will ask you to refer to both of the non-fiction texts. Question 2 will ask you to consider the similarities and/or differences between the two sources. Question 4 will ask you to consider how the two writers convey their different attitudes towards the same subject.

Read the extracts below and answer the questions.

Extract A from source 6b: from *The American Frugal Housewife* *(19th)*

'Time is money.' For this reason, cheap as stockings are, it is good economy to knit them. Cotton and woollen yarn[1] are both cheap; stockings that are knit wear twice as long as woven ones; and they can be done at odd minutes of time, which would not be otherwise employed. Where there are children, or aged people, it is sufficient to recommend knitting, that it is an employment.

Nothing should be thrown away so long as it is possible to make any use of it, however trifling that use may be; and whatever be the size of a family, every member should be employed either in earning or saving money.

1: yarn: thread used for knitting, weaving or sewing

Extract B from source 6a: 'Women aren't "better" at housework' *(21st)*

Housework is boring, so it makes sense that arguing about it – or trying to battle the gender inequality around it – would also be pretty mind-numbing. After spending a day picking up socks, no one really wants to talk about who picked up the socks.

But caring about equality across the board shouldn't be a zero sum game, and women are not going to be able to make progress on more urgent and public and political issues if we're too damn tired from doing so much work at home.

The texts in Paper 2 may be similar or different in various ways. Think about:
- the writers' points of view
- their context
- the language they use
- the writer's tone.

Guided 1 Write one similarity and one difference between Extract A and Extract B.

Similarity: ....

Difference: ....

Guided 2 Using your answers to Question 1, write two paragraphs comparing how the two writers convey their different attitudes towards housework.

....
....
....
....
....
....
....
....
....

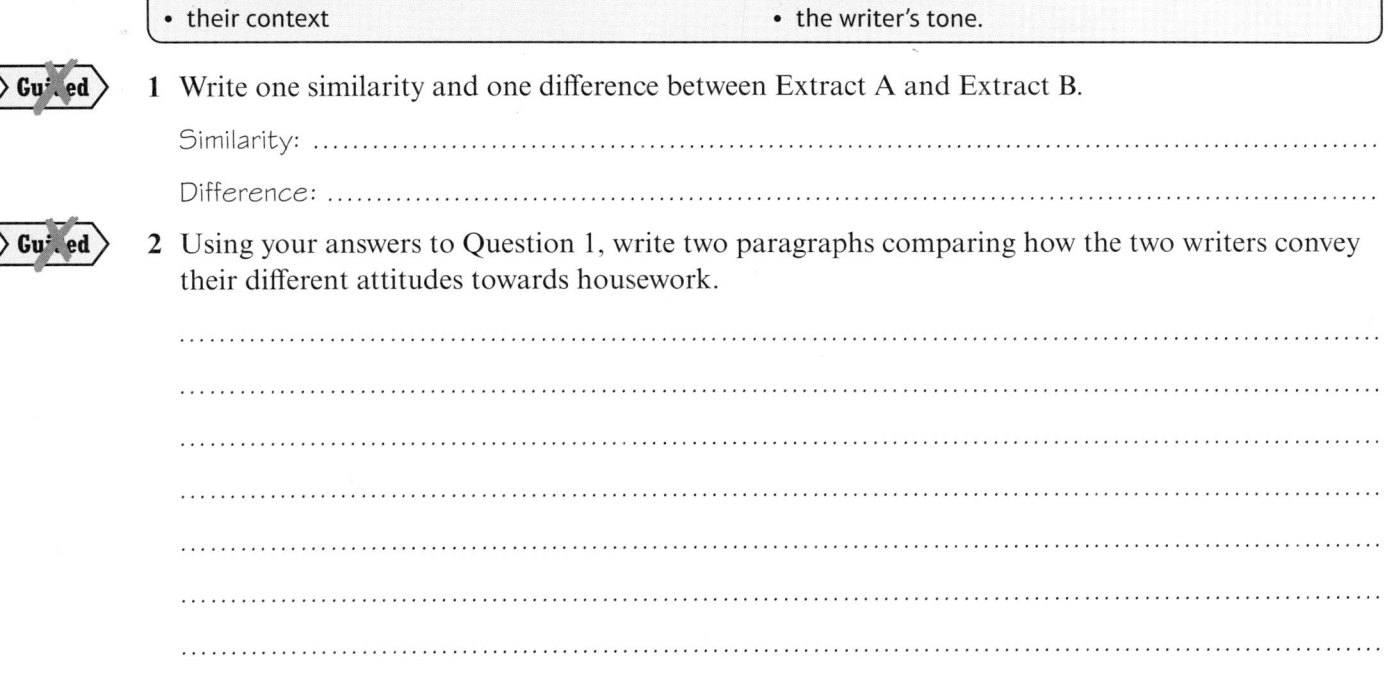

SECTION A READING Had a go ☐ Nearly there ☐ Nailed it! ☐

Selecting evidence for synthesis

When selecting information for the synthesis question (Question 2 in Paper 2), you need to choose evidence that is relevant to the question. Read the exam-style question below. **You don't need to answer this question.** Instead, think about what it is asking you to do, then answer Questions 1 and 2.

Paper 2

2 You need to refer to **source 7a** and **source 7b** for this question. Both sources give a description of a place that is haunted.
   Use details from **both** sources to write a summary of the differences. **(8 marks)**

Guided 1 Underline or highlight the key words in exam-style Question 2.

Guided 2 Look at the short extracts below. Which ones would be a good source of relevant quotations in answer to Question 2 above? Circle one extract from each text.

21st
   (a) Extracts from source 7a: 'Creating ghost stories'
   (i) Much depends on the mood we are in. At times of dread we are more receptive to stories and notions that may seem impossible, just as nightmares will visit more likely at such times.
   (ii) Like a simmering undercurrent this past lingers on into the present.

19th
   (b) Extracts from source 7b: 'Haunted Houses'
   (i) The new proprietor lost no time in sending for a glazier, and the mysterious noises ceased forever.
   (ii) Who has not either seen or heard of some house […] from which, at midnight, strange sounds have been heard to issue: the rattling of chains, and the groaning of perturbed spirits?

3 You might be asked about the similarities between sources for this question. Read the whole of **source 7a** on page 109 and **source 7b** on page 110. Draw a quick table of similarities and differences between the sources and then find relevant quotes to support your ideas. Some ideas have already been included in the table below.

	Source 7a	Source 7b
Positive/negative effects of imagination		
The past		
The atmosphere of a haunted place		

> As only 8 marks are available for the synthesis question, skim read the texts to save time.

Had a go ☐ Nearly there ☐ Nailed it! ☐

SECTION A READING

Answering a synthesis question

When you are synthesising the evidence you have selected from the two non-fiction texts in Paper 2, you need to use suitable adverbials and linking phrases.

1 Tick or circle the adverbials and linking phrases below that are suitable for finding **differences** between evidence. Two examples have been done for you.

   On the other hand   by contrast   (unlike)   both
   the same as   however   (yet)

2 Why should you use adverbials in your synthesis of evidence?

   Using adverbials helps you link together the similarities and/or the ....
   ....

   > Using adverbials makes it clear to your examiner that you are actually synthesising.

To show your full understanding of the synthesis question, you should start your answer with an overview. Read the exam-style question below. **You don't need to answer this question now.** Instead, think about what it is asking you to do, then answer Question 3.

Paper 2

> 2 You need to refer to **source 7a** and **source 7b** for this question. Use details from both sources. Write a summary of the differences between the haunted places.   **(8 marks)**

Guided

3 Tick the statements that you think you should include at the start of your answer.

   A Comments on both texts ☐
   B Quotations from the beginning ☐
   C Comparative adverbials or linking phrases ☐
   D A comparison of the attitudes in the texts ☐
   E A discussion of language techniques being used ☐
   F A statement that starts 'I will explain the attitudes' ☐
   G Reference to just one text ☐

Guided

4 Look at the overviews below, written by students in response to exam-style Question 2 above.

   > **A** The haunted place of Essex is made to sound exciting in source 7a unlike in source 7b.

   > **B** Both writers write about how scary haunted places are.

   > **C** In source 7a, Essex is made to sound exciting because it is haunted – the hauntings make it an enticing place. In source 7b, however, haunted houses are avoided because they are haunted – visitors are repelled from them.

   (a) Tick or circle the overview that you think is most effective.

   (b) Explain why the overview you have chosen would be the best way to start an answer to Question 2 above.

   ....
   ....

SECTION A READING

Had a go ☐   Nearly there ☐   Nailed it! ☐

Looking closely at language

Read these two short extracts from **source 7a**, 'Creating ghost stories', and **source 7b**, 'Haunted Houses', then answer Questions 1 and 2.

Extract A from source 7a: There has been so much personal terror, so much anguish, so much blood soaked into Essex soil, that it is perhaps not surprising that there are so many tales of hauntings, of supernatural sightings and unexplainable experiences. Can you imagine Valkyries[2] or witches riding in such a sky, on such a day?

2: Valkyries: Norse female warriors

Extract B from source 7b: Who has not either seen or heard of some house, shut up and uninhabitable, fallen into decay, and looking dusty and dreary, from which, at midnight, strange sounds have been heard to issue: the rattling of chains, and the groaning of perturbed spirits?

1 (a) Complete the table to compare the two extracts.

	Extract A	Extract B
Purpose		
Language		Alliteration – 'decay', 'dusty', 'dreary' – the pattern of three.
Technique	Rhetorical question:	

> When answering a comparison question in the exam, you should always look for similarities and differences between the language in the two texts. You must not write about one text without making a comparison point about the other. Try to give the texts equal weighting in your answer.

(b) Look at the 'Language' section of the table. Write how the uses of language differ.

The language used in Extract A is more fact based, whereas in Extract B the writer is more descriptive which creates an eerier atmosphere. ....

....

Both texts ....

....

2 Look at both sources. Both writers' use the rhetorical question. What is the effect of this technique in each extract?

Extract **A**   Extract **B**

....

....

> Think about what emotion the text is trying to conjure: is it sinister, descriptive, light-hearted? Also think about how it makes you feel: do you feel happy, apprehensive, scared?

Had a go ☐ Nearly there ☐ Nailed it! ☐

SECTION A READING

Planning to compare language

Read the extracts below, then complete the questions.

19th

Extract A from source 5b: 'The Boat to America'

My own two hands, and feet likewise, being very cold, however, on this particular occasion, I crept below at midnight. It was not exactly comfortable below. It was decidedly close; and it was impossible to be unconscious of the presence of that extraordinary compound of strange smells, which is to be found nowhere but on board ship, and which is such a subtle perfume that it seems to enter at every pore of the skin, and whisper of the hold.

21st

Extract B from source 5a: 'Googled your cough?'

You may think I sound crazy but, actually, I just have a mild form of cyberchondria: a condition in which benign aches and pains are transformed into fatal diseases after a few minutes spent looking up symptoms on Google. It's a common ailment[1]: one in 20 Google searches are health-related and, according to a 2012 study, one in four British women have misdiagnosed themselves on the internet.

1: ailment: sickness

1. Complete the table with ideas about how language is used in the two extracts to convey the writers' attitudes. The first one is done for you.

	Extract A	**Extract B**
Tone	The serious, formal tone — for example, 'I could not but observe' and 'notwithstanding' — suggests intelligence and experience.	The factual but informal tone shows that the writer is mocking the subject.
Rhetorical devices		
Use of imagery		

2. Using your completed table, write a few sentences comparing how the two writers use language to convey their viewpoints.

   Dickens uses descriptive language to convey his viewpoints by helping place the reader within the situation he is describing ....
   ....
   ....
   ....

> As well as comparing the writers' use of language, remember to also think about how their context and use of structure contribute to how their viewpoints are portrayed. When comparing you can:
> - start with the language and structural techniques the texts have in common, then compare the effects created
>
> OR
> - start with similarities in the effects of the two texts (for example, tone), then compare the techniques the writers have used to create those effects.

SECTION A READING

Had a go ☐   Nearly there ☐   Nailed it! ☐

Comparing language

Read Extracts A and B below. Then answer the questions that follow.

Extract A from source 6a: from *The American Frugal Housewife*

Buy merely enough to get along with at first. It is only by experience that you can tell what will be the wants of your family. If you spend all your money, you will find you have purchased many things you do not want, and have no means left to get many things which you do want.

Extract B from source 6a: 'Women aren't "better" at housework'

If your eyes are already starting to glaze over, you're not alone: every year, in every country, the same sort of statistics come out, and every year there are a few articles pointing out the disparity[1] and every year, in every country, nothing changes.

So women, let's remember that our unpaid labour is work too – and that we need to hold men accountable. Men … just do the damn dishes.

1: disparity: unfair difference/inequality

1   Two similar language features in the two extracts have been listed for you. For each feature, explain the effect they have.

(a) Imperatives: The writer sounds knowledgeable and ....
....
....

(b) Direct address: ....
....
....

> **Remember:**
> • Imperatives are sentences that give a command, instruction or advice, e.g. 'Keep off the grass'.
> • Direct address involves using the pronouns 'you', 'your' and 'you're' to involve the reader directly.

Guided   2 (a) Identify one purpose or effect of each extract from the choices below:

   A Create relationship with reader   E Instruct the reader
   B Persuade reader to agree   F Explain to the reader
   C Create humour   G Anger the reader
   D Frustrate the reader   H Make the reader cry

(b) What is the language technique used in Extract A to achieve this effect?

Extract A: Repetition of the word ....
....
....

(c) What is the language technique used in Extract B to achieve this effect?

Extract B: ....
....
....

44

Had a go ☐   Nearly there ☐   Nailed it! ☐

SECTION A READING

Comparing structure

You can compare viewpoints of a text by analysing its structure. Structural techniques assist the writer in portraying the desired perspective.

1 Look at the opening and concluding paragraphs of two extracts and add notes to the table below.

Extract A: 'Googled your cough?'

Opening paragraph

At 11am I had a strange pain in my toe. By 11.05 I was convinced it was a brain tumour. By 11.15 I'd realised that, actually, my shoes were probably to blame, but by that time I'd already decided on the music that should be played at my funeral.

Extract B: 'The Boat to America'

We all dined together that day; and a rather formidable[1] party we were: no fewer than eighty-six strong. The vessel being pretty deep in the water, with all her coals on board and so many passengers, and the weather being calm and quiet, there was but little motion…

1: formidable: impressive/intimidating

Conclusion

Indeed, it's possible that, by now, you are starting to remember that your toe hurts, or you have a headache, or your leg is twitching. You may feel an urge to Google your symptoms. Hypochondriacs, please proceed with caution.

Now every plank and timber creaked, as if the ship were made of wicker-work; and now crackled, like an enormous fire of the driest possible twigs. There was nothing for it but bed; so I went to bed.

		Structural techniques	Effect
Opening paragraph	Extract A		
	Extract B	• Long descriptive sentences • Subordinate clauses • First person narration • Personal perspective	
Concluding paragraph	Extract A		
	Extract B		

> **Guided**

2 Choose either the opening paragraph or the conclusion. Use your notes from the table above and write a paragraph comparing how the texts are structured and how this has an impact on the reader.

....
....
....
....
....

Comparing ideas

SECTION A — READING | Had a go ☐ | Nearly there ☐ | Nailed it! ☐

Read the openings of 'The Boat to America' and 'Googled your cough?' below.

> **Extract A from source 5b: 'The Boat to America'**
> Two passengers' wives (one of them my own) lay already in silent agonies on the sofa; and one lady's maid (*my lady's*) was a mere bundle on the floor, cursing her destiny. Everything sloped the wrong way: which in itself was an aggravation[10] scarcely to be borne.

> Writers craft their writing deliberately. They use a range of techniques and methods in order to achieve their desired effect and create an impact on the reader.

10: aggravation: annoyance

> **Extract B from source 5a: 'Googled your cough?'**
> But Google's medical intervention isn't without serious side-effects. First, it gives Google even more control over the information we consume every day. Second, by making it easier to research medical conditions, this new function is basically crack cocaine for healthy worriers.

1 Use your language and structural comparison skills to explain how the main **ideas** are presented in the extracts. Complete the table and then circle whether the extracts are similar or different in their use of the techniques. One has been done for you.

	Extract A	Extract B	Similar or different?
Main idea	The very real, personal experience of seasickness	Addictive, imagined illness	Similar/**different**
Language and effect	The writer uses figurative language to	....	Similar/different
Structure and effect	....	....	Similar/different

2 P–E–E paragraphs are a good way to structure your answer to a comparison question. Complete the table to show how the writers convey their ideas.

	Extract A	Extract B
Idea/point	Dickens creates an atmosphere of disorder	Googling symptoms is very addictive
Evidence	Dickens uses the phrase everything sloped the wrong way	....
Explanation	....	....

Guided **3** Write the next paragraph of the student's answer.

....
....
....
....

> Remember to use comparative linking phrases, and discuss the texts side by side rather than one after the other.

Had a go ☐ Nearly there ☐ Nailed it! ☐

SECTION A READING

Comparing perspective

Read the extracts below which are the opening paragraphs of two texts about housework. Then answer Questions 1 and 2.

19th

Extract A from source 6b: *The American Frugal Housewife*
The true economy of housekeeping is simply the art of gathering up all the fragments, so that nothing be lost. I mean fragments of time, as well as materials.

21st

Extract B from source 6a: 'Women aren't "better" at housework'
Housework is boring, so it makes sense that arguing about it – or trying to battle the gender inequality around it – would also be pretty mind-numbing. After spending a day picking up socks, no one really wants to talk about who picked up the socks.

Guided

1 Compare how the viewpoints on housework differ in the opening sentences.

....

....

....

> Remember to use adverbials (such as 'like', 'also', 'both' and 'by contrast') to make links between the texts.

2 (a) What language techniques does the writer of **Extract B** use to show their perspective?

In *The American Frugal Housewife*, the writer uses formal language, such as 'so that nothing be lost', to show strong feelings about avoiding waste in the home. ....

....

....

(b) How does this differ from **Extract A**?

....

....

Read the full extracts from *The American Frugal Housewife,* in **source 6b**, on page 108, and 'Women aren't "better" at housework', in **source 6a** on page 107. Pay particular attention to the way they end. Then answer Question 3.

Guided

3 Compare the endings of each extract. Have perspectives remained the same or do they end with a different point of view? Use one piece of evidence from each of the sources.

....

....

....

....

....

> It is important when comparing perspectives to look at the beginning and the ending of a text. Analysing the structure of a text is also helpful when looking at differences in viewpoint.

47

SECTION A READING

Had a go ☐ Nearly there ☐ Nailed it! ☐

Answering a comparison question

Read the two extracts below. Then answer Questions 1 and 2.

[21st]

Extract A from source 7a: 'Creating ghost stories'

And in an otherwise empty landscape of a tidal marsh with only crustaceans and seagulls for witnesses, the mewling cry of some seabirds might well be mistaken for something more sinister in half-light or mist.

What dastardly crime could be waiting in such a setting? What could be lurking down that path? Could that be where the body was hidden?

[19th]

Extract B from source 7b: 'Haunted Houses'

Who has not either seen or heard of some house, shut up and uninhabitable, fallen into decay, and looking dusty and dreary, from which, at midnight, strange sounds have been heard to issue: the rattling of chains, and the groaning of perturbed[1] spirits? [...]

The gossips of the neighbourhood asserted that they often heard groans from the cellars, and saw lights moved about from one window to the other immediately after the midnight bell had tolled.

1: perturbed: anxious or unsettled

1 Complete the table of techniques that you can write about in a comparison question. Include evidence from the texts as an example.

	Example	Extract A	Extract B	Different or similar effect?
Language and structure	• Repetition • Rhetorical question • Alliteration			
Perspective	Optimistic or pessimistic		Negative language and imagery –	
Effect on the reader	• Fear • Humour • Intrigue • Persuasion			

> In Paper 2, you could focus on one language or structural feature or its effect in the first text, then compare it to a similar feature or effect in the second text.

> Remember that is important to understand what each text is about before you start comparing how they achieve that effect.

Guided 2 Choose one language or structural feature and its effect in Extract A, then compare it to a similar feature and effect in Extract B.

....

....

....

> Remember to make direct comparisons, using adverbials such as 'unlike', 'also', 'both' and 'by contrast'. Also, remember that you can compare similarities **and** differences between the two texts.

Had a go ☐ Nearly there ☐ Nailed it! ☐

SECTION A READING

Putting it into practice

Guided

Read 'Women aren't "better" at housework', in **source 6a** on page 107, and *The American Frugal Housewife,* in **source 6b** on page 108, then answer the exam-style question below.

Paper 2

4 For this question, you need to refer to the **whole of source 6a** together with **source 6b**. Compare how the two writers convey their different attitudes to housework.

In your answer, you could:
- compare their different attitudes
- compare the methods they use to convey their attitudes
- support your ideas with quotations from both texts.

(16 marks)

> When you tackle this type of question in the exam, remember to:
> - spend about 20 minutes on your answer
> - read the question carefully and highlight the main focus
> - spend a couple of minutes planning your answer before you start writing
> - always write about both texts throughout your answer
> - identify the language and structural devices used and comment on how they help the writer to get across their ideas and arguments.

> **Remember:** You have more space than this to answer your question in the exam. Use your own paper to finish your answer to the question above.

SECTION B WRITING Had a go ☐ Nearly there ☐ Nailed it! ☐

Writing questions: an overview

Both papers of the English Language GCSE include a writing section: Section B.

1 Read the statement below, and decide which paper is being described by each statement (some may describe both papers). Circle your choices.

(a) The focus is on descriptive and/or narrative writing.	**(Paper 1)** Paper 2
(b) The focus is on presenting a particular view or argument.	Paper 1 **(Paper 2)**
(c) It tests your ability to write for different purposes or audiences.	Paper 1 Paper 2
(d) It tests your ability to write imaginatively and creatively.	Paper 1 Paper 2
(e) You have a choice of writing question.	Paper 1 Paper 2

Assessment objective 5
(a) (Communicate) clearly, effectively and imaginatively, selecting and adapting tone, style and register for different forms, purposes and audiences
(b) (Organise) information and ideas, using structural and grammatical features to support coherence and cohesion of texts

Assessment objective 6
Use a range of (vocabulary) and sentence (structures) for clarity, purpose and effect, with accurate spelling and punctuation

2 Next, read the statements about the assessment objectives and circle which you are being tested on (some may describe both assessment objectives).

(a) Tests whether you can use a wide range of well-chosen vocabulary.	AO5 **(AO6)**
(b) Tests whether you can organise your writing clearly, and signpost the reader.	**(AO5)** AO6
(c) Tests whether you can use accurate grammar and sentence structures.	AO5 AO6
(d) Tests whether you can use a range of complex punctuation to create deliberate effect.	AO5 AO6
(e) Tests whether you can write for a given audience, form and purpose.	AO5 AO6
(f) Tests whether you can communicate imaginatively.	AO5 AO6

3 Summarise each assessment objective into one short sentence without using the words that are circled in the descriptions above.

Assessment objective 5 (a)
Write ....

Assessment objective 5 (b)
Arrange ....

Assessment objective 6
Use ....

Be ....

Had a go ☐   Nearly there ☐   Nailed it! ☐

SECTION B WRITING

Writing questions: Paper 1

Paper 1 tests your creative writing skills.

1. Read the statements about Paper 1 below. Identify which is true or false, and circle your choice.

   (a) You need to write either a description or a narrative.   **(True)**   False

   (b) You can write a poem.   True   False

   (c) You can write a play.   True   False

   (d) There may be an image to describe.   True   False

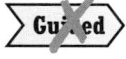

Guided

2. Which of the terms below is another word for 'narrative'? Circle your answer.

   Speech   Story   Description   Article

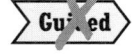

Guided

3. Think about the definitions of 'describe' and 'narrate'. Identify which term applies to the following skills (both may apply to some skills):

   (a) Uses a series of plot points or events   Describe   Narrate

   (b) Uses the senses to create a vivid atmosphere   Describe   Narrate

   (c) Creates a strong atmosphere   Describe   Narrate

   (d) Based on a single scene   Describe   Narrate

   (e) Uses the prompt as a starting point   Describe   Narrate

4. Look at the exam-style question below. **You don't need to answer this question.** Instead, consider its form, purpose and audience. Complete the table by adding in the responses that would be suitable for this task – there might be more than one response for each.

Paper 1

5. You are going to enter a creative writing competition. Your entry will be judged by your classmates.

   Either:

   Write a description suggested by the picture.

   Or:

   Write the opening part of a story about doing something frightening.

   (40 marks)

Form	Description	Story opening
Purpose		Set the scene and to draw the reader in
Audience		

SECTION B WRITING

Had a go ☐   Nearly there ☐   Nailed it! ☐

Writing questions: Paper 2

Paper 2 tests your skills in writing to present a viewpoint.

Guided

1 When writing to present a viewpoint, you will need to write in a certain way. Circle the words that represent the writing form you should use.

argue   inform   describe   narrate   persuade   explain

> Here's a quick reminder of what each form means:
> - Argue – give your opinion and state why the opposite view is wrong
> - Inform – give facts about a subject
> - Describe – give a description of what someone or something is like
> - Narrate – write a story
> - Persuade – give a one-sided opinion which convinces the reader
> - Explain – give detailed information about a topic.

Look at the Paper 2 exam-style question below. **You don't need to answer this question**. Instead, consider what it is asking you to do, then answer Question 2.

Paper 2

5 'Surfing the internet is pointless. Time spent browsing online could be used doing something else worthwhile.'

Write an article for your local newspaper in which you explain your point of view on this statement.

(40 marks)

Guided

2 (a) Circle the word(s) in the exam-style question that tell you which **audience** (the people this is aimed at) you should be writing for.

(b) Circle the word(s) in the exam-style question that tell you the **form** (the type of writing, e.g. letter, speech) the answer should take.

(c) Circle the word(s) in the exam-style question that tell you what the **purpose** (e.g. argue, inform) of your writing should be.

3 Plan an answer for the exam-style Question 5. Consider the positives and negatives of spending time browsing (looking at things) online. Write your notes in bullet points below. One example for each has been completed for you:

> It is a good idea to do a quick table or mind map using the headings 'positives' and 'negatives'. This will help you organise your ideas.

- Positive 1. Lots of educational websites help pupils with their homework and revision.
- Positive 2. ....
- Positive 3. ....
- Positive 4. ....
- Negative 1. Social media is a distraction; you can waste hours chatting with friends.
- Negative 2. ....
- Negative 3. ....
- Negative 4. ....

Had a go ☐ Nearly there ☐ Nailed it! ☐

SECTION B WRITING

Writing questions: time management

The table below shows the three key stages to complete when answering a Paper 1 or a Paper 2 writing task.

1. Complete the table by writing in the number of minutes you should spend on each stage. The first row has been done for you.

	Paper 1, Section B: Writing	Paper 2, Section B: Writing
Total time	45 minutes	45 minutes
Planning your answer		
Writing your answer		
Checking and proofreading your answer		

2. Now match each description and number of minutes to the correct part of the time management pie chart.

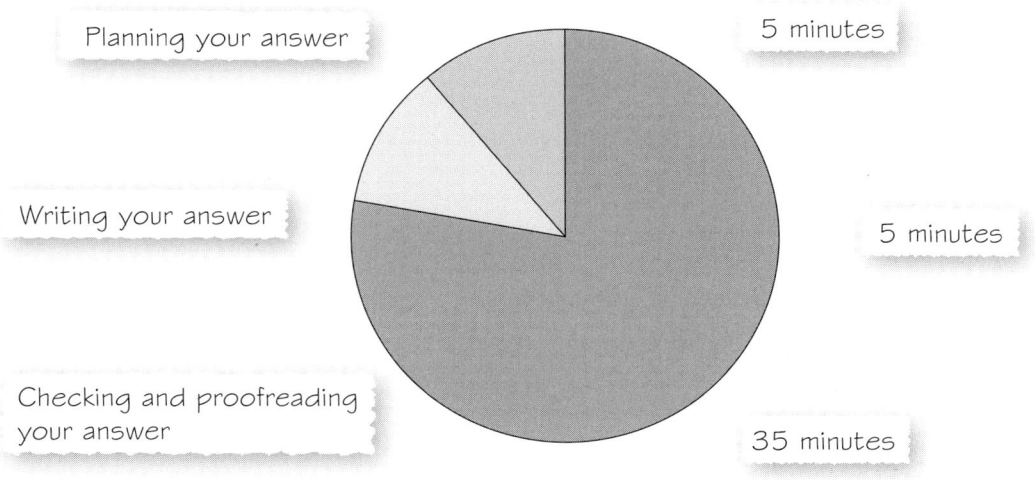

Planning your answer

5 minutes

Writing your answer

5 minutes

Checking and proofreading your answer

35 minutes

Guided

3. Read the statements about the writing task below. Decide whether each statement is true or false. Circle your choices.

   (a) Keep writing till the end, even if it means finishing halfway through a sentence.   **True   False**

   (b) Conclusions are important.   **True   False**

   (c) Don't pause during the writing as you might lose marks.   **True   False**

   (d) You should spend the same amount of time on Section A as on Section B.   **True   False**

   (e) Use bullets to express your remaining ideas if you run out of time.   **True   False**

   (f) Write a note to the examiner letting them know you have run out of time.   **True   False**

4. During the writing process, what are six questions you can ask yourself to help you with time management? List your ideas below. Two have been completed for you.

   (a) Am I still writing in the correct form?

   (b) Will my target reader be engaged by this?

   (c) ....

   (d) ....

   (e) ....

   (f) ....

SECTION B WRITING Had a go ☐   Nearly there ☐   Nailed it! ☐

Writing for a purpose: creative 1

Look at the exam-style question below. **Don't answer this question now.** Think about what you might include in a response, then answer Questions 1 to 4.

Paper ①

> 5 You have been asked to write a creative piece for a local magazine. Describe a visit to a local landmark or important place. **(40 marks)**

> AO5 asks you to write 'imaginatively', which can include creating a vivid atmosphere or feeling.

1 Using the senses can help to create a vivid atmosphere. Complete the table below, gathering ideas for the exam-style question above. Some ideas have been added for you.

See	
Hear	Laughing children in the water fountain
Smell	
Touch	
Taste	Chocolate flake melting into ice-cream

2 Writing a description that *shows* emotions or ideas is more engaging than just telling them because the reader becomes more involved in the writing. Complete the table below to suggest some ways these ideas could be *shown* rather than *told*.

He was angry.	
She was nervous.	Her fingers drummed a quick rhythm on the table, waiting.
It was a hot day.	
She was thirsty.	She licked her cracked lips.
They were happy.	

Guided 3 Figurative language also helps to develop description and vivid images. Using the idea of a cold place, write an imaginative example that you could use in a response to the exam-style question above.

Simile	
Metaphor	
Personification	

> Remember that using a few well-chosen phrases is better than using many unimaginative ones.

4 Writing strong verbs can help with descriptive writing. Replace these verbs and adverbs with single verbs. Some have been suggested for you.

Walking quickly	Skipping, running, pacing
Closed the door firmly	
Shouted angrily	Hollered

5 Write the first three sentences of your answer to the exam-style question. Use your answers to Questions 1 to 4. Remember to choose your vocabulary carefully, and show ideas rather telling them.

The castle was as ....
....
....

Had a go ☐   Nearly there ☐   Nailed it! ☐

SECTION B WRITING

Writing for a purpose: creative 2

Read the exam-style question below. **You don't need to answer this yet.** Instead, think about what it is asking you to do, then read the opening section of one student's response and answer Questions 1 to 3.

Paper 1

> 5 You have entered a creative writing competition, which will be judged by people your own age. Write the opening of a story starting with the line 'I didn't mean it.'   **(40 marks)**

> I didn't mean it. The park lights were on, little puddles of light on the ground, but everything else melted into darkness. My hands shook like jelly and I was afraid. Jess was next to me at first. We walked down the path nervously, each of us thinking our own thoughts. I don't want to go through with what we had agreed.

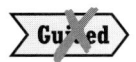

Guided

1 The student answer uses techniques to create an engaging narrative. Underline and annotate the text showing evidence of the following:
- feelings
- the five senses
- figurative language
- language choice

2 What advice would you give the student on the following sections?

Think about any clichés the student might have used.

(a) 'My hands shook like jelly and I was afraid.'

Shows ....

....

(b) '… melted into darkness'.

The common metaphor ....

....

(c) 'We walked down the path nervously, each of us thinking our own thoughts.'

The adverb ....

....

(d) 'I don't want to go through with what we had agreed'

The present tense ....

....

3 Why do the following sections work well to create a vivid opening?

(a) 'little puddles of light on the ground'

The metaphor suggests ....

....

(b) 'Jess was next to me at first'

This creates a sense that ....

....

(c) 'I don't want to go through with what we had agreed'

Hints at what is to come ....

....

SECTION B WRITING Had a go ☐ Nearly there ☐ Nailed it! ☐

Writing for a purpose: viewpoint 1

Look at the exam-style question below. **You don't need to answer this question.** Instead, think about what you might include in a response to this question, then answer Questions 1 to 4.

> 5 'Young drivers are a danger to other road users.'
>
> Write an article for a newspaper in which you explain your point of view on this statement.
>
> **(40 marks)**

1 Decide whether you want to write for or against the newspaper's suggestion. Write down three key points to support your point of view. An example *for* the statement has been done for you, but you can choose to write against it if you prefer.

   Example point: Younger drivers usually take greater risks when behind the wheel.

   Point 1: ....

   Point 2: ....

2 Write down a piece of evidence to support each of the points in your answer to Question 1. An example has been done for you.

   Example evidence: Young people are more likely to go over the speed limit.

   Evidence for point 1: ....

   Evidence for point 2: ....

> Evidence could be facts or statistics, an expert opinion or an example from your personal experience. The evidence you use in your writing in the exam does not have to be real or true, but it must be believable.

3 A counter-argument allows you to dismiss an opposing point of view. Think about the points you made in response to Question 1 above. What opposing points might somebody on the other side of the argument make? How could you dismiss them? Write down your ideas.

   Some people might feel ....

   ....

   However, ...

   ....

4 Rhetorical devices can strengthen your argument. Look at the list of devices below, then read the model answer. Underline and annotate the model answer to show the rhetorical devices used.

| rhetorical questions | direct address | repetition | lists | alliteration |
| contrast | pattern of three | emotive language | hyperbole | |

Some people might feel that young people will only become better drivers with practice. However, it is clear from the statistics about road accidents involving young drivers that they are more likely to be involved in a serious crash, more likely to speed and more likely to overtake on blind corners. Knowing these facts, would you be willing for a young driver to drive your car? Many people might not have the same patience for young people to practise on the roads if one was involved in a deadly crash with someone they cared about.

Had a go ☐ Nearly there ☐ Nailed it! ☐

SECTION B WRITING

Writing for a purpose: viewpoint 2

Look at the exam-style question below. **You don't need to answer this question now**. Instead, think about what you might include in a response to this statement, then answer Questions 1 to 3.

Paper ②

> 5 'Mobile phones should be banned in all schools.'
>
> Write an article for your school magazine explaining your point of view on this statement.
> **(40 marks)**

1 Writing that informs and explains often uses headings and subheadings to guide the reader and make the information easier to find. List up to three subheadings that you could use to organise your answer to the exam-style question. An example has been done for you.

(a) Distraction in lessons

(b) ....

(c) ....

2 Using facts and statistics is an effective way to make your writing appear credible. Fill out the table below with three facts or statistics that you could include under your headings and the point they will be supporting. An example has been done for you.

Fact	Point
Test scores rise by 6% in schools where mobiles aren't allowed.	Banning mobiles in schools means students would get higher grades.

3 There are other techniques that you can use to inform and explain in your writing. Using your responses from Question 1 and 2, make notes on how you would use each of the techniques below.

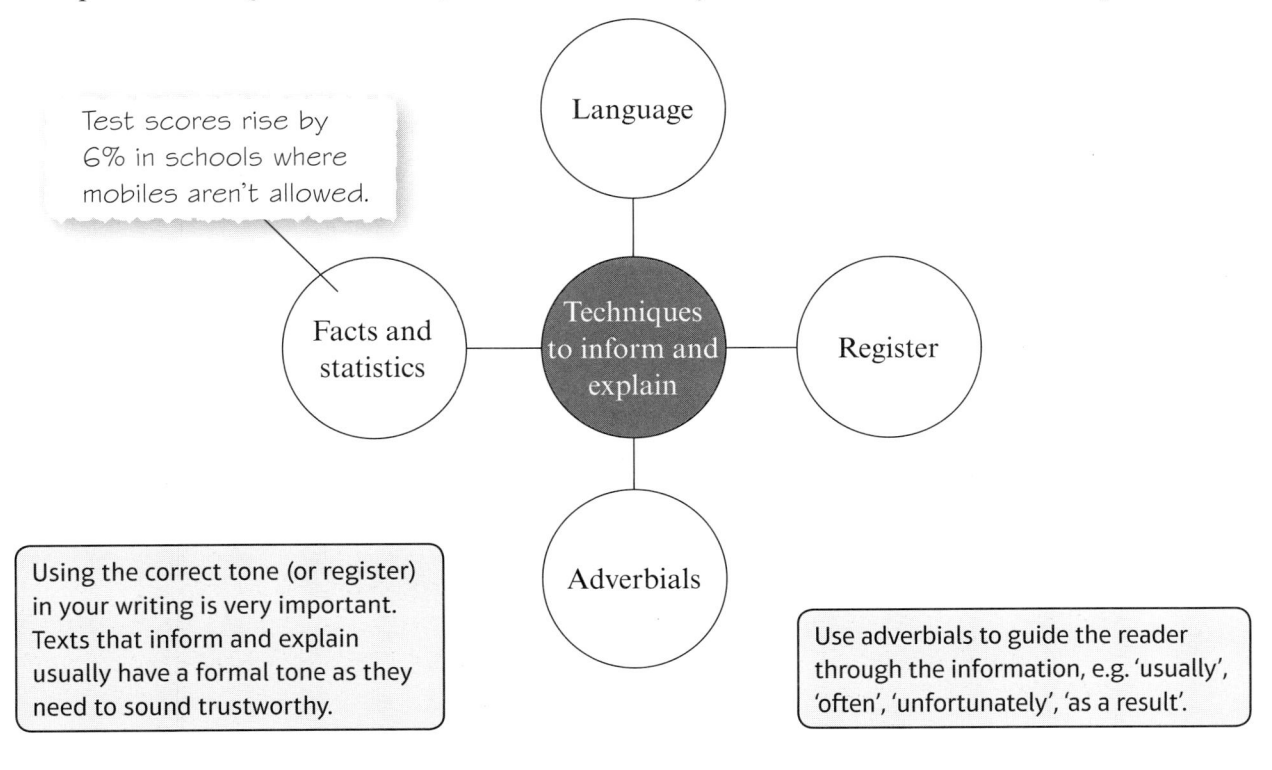

Test scores rise by 6% in schools where mobiles aren't allowed. → Facts and statistics

Techniques to inform and explain:
- Language
- Facts and statistics
- Register
- Adverbials

Using the correct tone (or register) in your writing is very important. Texts that inform and explain usually have a formal tone as they need to sound trustworthy.

Use adverbials to guide the reader through the information, e.g. 'usually', 'often', 'unfortunately', 'as a result'.

57

SECTION B WRITING

Had a go ☐   Nearly there ☐   Nailed it! ☐

Writing for an audience

Some Paper 2 writing questions will clearly state the audience you should write for. Others will only hint at the audience. Look at the exam-style question below. **You don't need to answer it.** Instead, think about what you might include in a response to this statement, then answer Questions 1 and 2.

Paper 2

5 'Movies these days are too violent and include too much swearing.'
   Write an article for a broadsheet newspaper explaining your point of view on
   this statement. **(40 marks)**

> Remember, broadsheet newspapers (such as *The Guardian* or *The Times*) have large sheets and focus on serious issues.

1 Describe the implied audience for this piece of writing. Include your thoughts on age and gender.

   The audience is likely to be ....

   ....

   ....

Guided

2 Look at the following sentence. Does it have an appropriate tone and vocabulary for the audience you identified in Question 1? Rewrite it to improve it.

   The films kids watch on the telly might be full of filthy language but I reckon they are still top entertainment.

   ....

   ....

> Think about formal and informal words when writing for your audience. For example, 'kids' could become 'children'.

Now look at this exam-style question. **You don't need to answer this question now.** Instead, think about the language you might use in your response, then answer Question 3.

Paper 2

5 'Doing homework is often a waste of time and effort.'
   Write a speech for teachers, explaining your point of view on this statement. **(40 mark)**

3 An answer to exam-style Question 5 has been started for you below. Add two sentences to this opening.

   Let's be clear. The homework you set is often demotivating. Especially when you don't bother to mark it! If you really want us to complete homework, you might want to consider setting us something innovative and interesting. Then we'll be keen to get stuck in. ....

   ....

   ....

   ....

   ....

Had a go ☐   Nearly there ☐   Nailed it! ☐

SECTION B WRITING

Putting it into practice

Read the exam-style question below. **You don't need to answer this question.** Instead, think about the descriptive and narrative options, and what these might involve. Then answer Questions 1 and 2.

Paper 1

5 A local writing competition for teenagers is looking for entries.

Either:

Write a description suggested by this picture.

Or:

Write the opening of a story about a shipwreck.

(40 marks)

When you tackle this kind of question in the exam, remember to:
- plan your time – you have 45 minutes for this question, including planning and checking
- read the question carefully and decide which option to answer
- plan your writing, including ideas about narrative or descriptive techniques you might use
- make sure the form you choose is either a narrative or a description
- make sure you stick to the same narrative voice throughout your writing.

1 Plan the content for your chosen option by annotating the spider diagram below.

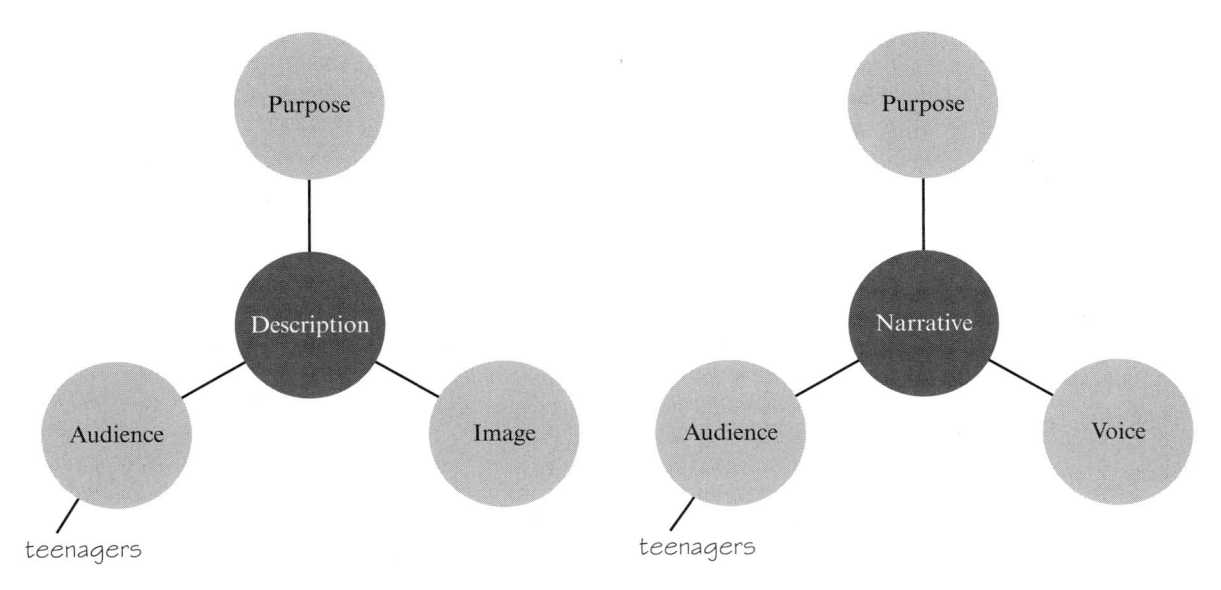

Description: Purpose, Audience (teenagers), Image

Narrative: Purpose, Audience (teenagers), Voice

Guided

2 Note down some ideas about descriptive techniques you could use in your answer. Write a sentence giving an example of each technique. One example has been done for you.

Technique 1: Personification

Example 1: The boat hurtled over the waves, its timbers creaking with every effort.

Technique 2: ....

Example 2: ....

SECTION B WRITING

Had a go ☐   Nearly there ☐   Nailed it! ☐

Putting it into practice

Read the exam-style question below. **You don't need to answer it.** Instead, think about what it is asking you to do, then complete the table.

Paper ②

5 'Only three schoolchildren should be allowed in shops at any one time.'

Write an article for your local newspaper in which you argue for or against this statement.

(40 marks)

> When you tackle this kind of question in the exam, remember to:
> - plan your time – you have 45 minutes to answer it, including planning and checking
> - read the question carefully
> - annotate the question to highlight the form, audience and purpose
> - plan your writing.

1 Plan a response to the exam-style question above by completing the table. A section has been completed for you.

Timing	Plan: .... minutes
	Write: .... minutes
	Check: .... minutes
Topic	
Form	
Audience	Probably adults of both genders
Purpose	
Two points for my argument	1 .... 2 ....
One point against my argument	1 ....
Any other key features	....

Had a go ☐   Nearly there ☐   Nailed it! ☐

SECTION B WRITING

Form: articles

Read the Paper 2 exam-style question below. **You don't need to answer this question.**
Instead, think about what it is asking you to do, then answer Questions 1 to 4.

Paper 2

> 5 'Surfing the internet is pointless. Time spent browsing online could be used doing something else worthwhile.'
>
> Write an article for your local newspaper explaining your point of view on this statement.
>
> **(40 marks)**

> Remember that you analysed this question on page 52. Look back to see the work you did on this page to help you answer this exam-style question.

1 Look at list of headlines that could be used for this article.
   Pick which you think is the best one and explain why.

   A   Only complete morons go on the internet.

   B   Stuck to your screen? Why the web is a waste of time.

   C   My article about surfing the internet.

   Headline .... is the best because ....
   ....

   > Headlines use a range of techniques including: repetition, a rhetorical question, alliteration, a pun or a rhyme.

Guided 2 Think of a subheading that will add more information to your headline.
   ....
   ....

3 Write your opening paragraph, summing up your ideas in two or three sentences.
   Many of us spend hours every day surfing the internet ....
   ....
   ....

4 Articles often use quotations from experts to make the information seem factual and reliable.
   Who could you quote in this article? What would they say?

   > Remember that the quotations or evidence you use in your writing in the exam do not have to be real or true, but they must be believable.

   Professor John Smith from Bristol University says ....
   ....
   ....
   ....

SECTION B WRITING

Had a go ☐   Nearly there ☐   Nailed it! ☐

Form: letters and reports

Read the Paper 2 exam-style question below. **You don't need to answer this question.** Instead, think about what you might need to include in your response, then answer Question 1.

Paper 2

5 'Shops and supermarkets should not be allowed to open on Sundays.'

Write an email to your local newspaper explaining your point of view on this statement. **(40 marks)**

1 The start of a student's response is included below and the mistakes have been underlined. Use the sample response to complete the table. One has been done for you.

> From: Ihateschool@emails.com
>
> Subject: <u>Stores shd b open on Sundays</u>
>
> Dear Sir/Madam,
>
> <u>Tons of</u> supermarket staff believe that the stores should be closed on Sundays. I believe that's <u>a load of rubbish;</u> since some people can only visit the shops on that day. <u>However,</u> many shop <u>owners'</u> will need to open on Sundays in order to make more money. Surely that should be <u>there</u> choice! This includes the shop on my road <u>where I always get a bar of chocolate if I go in after school</u>.
>
> <u>Yours sincerely,</u>
>
> Tom Banks

Informal language	Incorrect use of word	Incorrect punctuation	Irrelevant information
Ihateschool@emails.com			

> When answering a question of this type, remember to think about why someone would make the effort to write a letter to their newspaper. They will usually be annoyed by a statement in the newspaper. The answer should make this clear using tone but the writing should be kept formal.

Now read the following Paper 2 exam-style question. **You don't need to answer this question.** Instead, think about what might be needed for this piece of writing, then answer Question 2.

Paper 2

5 'School uniform should be free to all pupils.'

Write a report for your head teacher in which you explain your point of view on this statement. **(40 marks)**

Guided

2 Reports need to be formal and factual. An example headline for the report in exam-style Question 5 is below. Improve the headline, and then improve it again.

> Headline: I hate school uniforms!!!

> People will read your article because they are interested in the subject, so don't forget to keep on topic.

Improvement 1: ....

Improvement 2: ....

Had a go ☐   Nearly there ☐   Nailed it! ☐

SECTION B WRITING

Form: speeches

The techniques below are examples of what you could include to create an effective speech.

Guided

1. Match the techniques with the example provided.

   (a) Direct appeal to the listener

   (b) Use of emotive language to effectively express ideas

   (c) Range of facts and opinions to support viewpoint

   (d) Addresses challenges and offers solutions

   (e) Use of repetition to reinforce viewpoint

   (f) Use of personal examples to illustrate opinion

   (g) Use of short, direct statements

   (h) Use of rhetorical questions to encourage and provoke listener to engage in the debate

   A   Just this week, I spoke to a mother who told me, 'My child was left traumatised after watching a terrifying horror movie'.

   B   Young drivers become safe through experience. Experience comes only through practice.

   C   Mobile phones may be a distraction for some, yet I find mine a valuable source of information; looking up words in an online dictionary boosts my vocabulary.

   D   The boredom and frustration felt by young people with nothing to do in their area must be taken into account.

   E   Think of the planet and consider the future. Now is the time to rescue our environment.

   F   Respected teachers, I hope you will listen to my concerns about what this will do to your pupils.

   G   I appreciate that recycling would take more time and effort. But households could be helped with clear guidance and a combined recycling bin.

   H   How can you sit there and ignore this critical issue?

2. Read the following Paper 2 exam-style question below and plan a speech. Use the techniques above to help with putting together your plan.

Paper 2

5 'Sports stars are poor role models for young people.'

Write a speech for a youth group in which you explain your point of view on this statement.   **(40 marks)**

Who do you look up to? Who are your heroes? ....

....

....

....

....

....

....

63

SECTION B WRITING

Had a go ☐   Nearly there ☐   Nailed it! ☐

Putting it into practice

Answer the exam-style question below. Focus in particular on purpose, audience and form.

5 'Pupils spend too long sitting at desks. Each lesson should include a break for physical activity.'

Write a report for your headteacher in which you argue for or against this statement. **(40 marks)**

> When you tackle this type of question in the exam, remember to:
> - read the question carefully and identify the topic, form, audience and purpose of the writing
> - plan your writing before you start
> - include all the relevant key features of the form and purpose
> - spend 45 minutes on your answer, including planning and checking time.

> **Remember:** You are only being asked to write part of an answer on this page. In the exam, you will be give more space to write a full answer.

Had a go ☐   Nearly there ☐   Nailed it! ☐

SECTION B WRITING

Ideas and planning: creative

Read the exam-style question below. **You don't need to answer this question**. Instead, consider the question options then answer Questions 1 and 2.

Paper 1

> 5 Your local newspaper is inviting entries for a competition.
> **Either:**
> Write a description suggested by this picture.
>
> **Or:**
> Write a story about arriving in an unfamiliar city.
>
> **(40 marks)**

Guided

1 Write down your initial ideas for the descriptive option as either a list or a spider diagram.

> In the exam, you will have to write either a description or a narration. You might not have a choice which type of writing you do, but if you do, you'll need to choose the option quickly so that you don't waste planning time.

2 Now, look at a student's plan for the title 'Starting somewhere new'. Annotate the plan on the subject of 'senses', including ideas about creative writing techniques you could use.

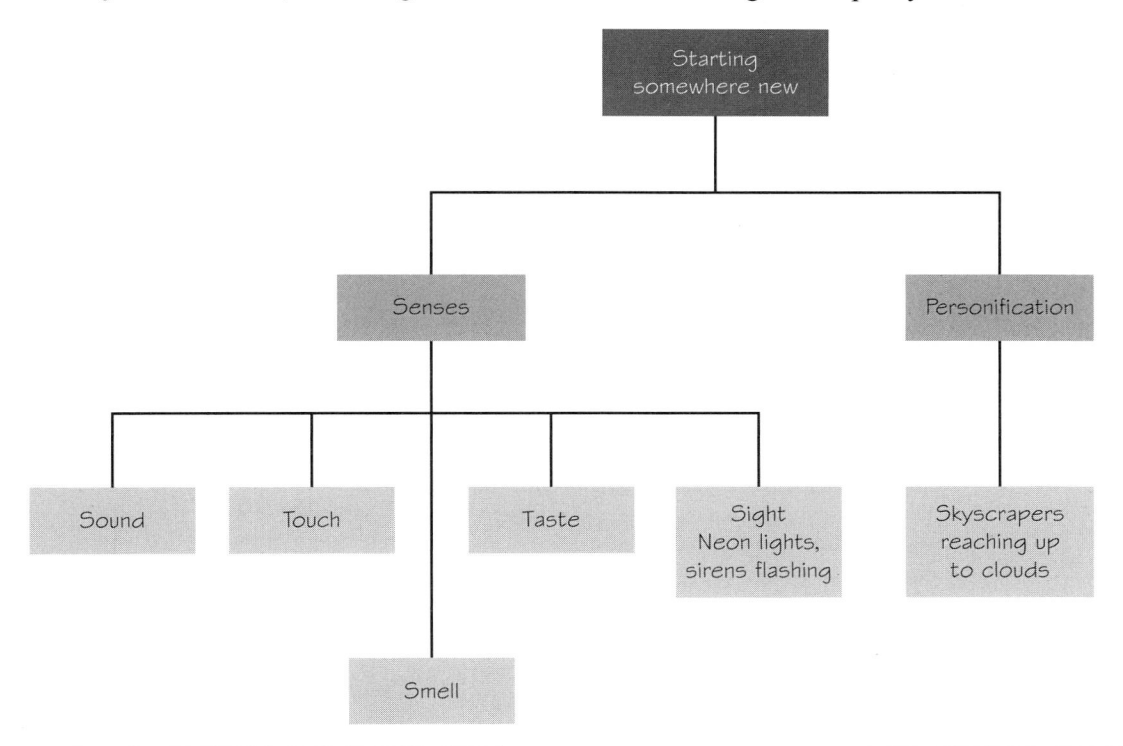

```
                    Starting
                  somewhere new
                        |
           ┌────────────┴────────────┐
         Senses                  Personification
           |                          |
   ┌───┬───┼───┬──────┐               |
 Sound Touch Taste  Sight        Skyscrapers
                  Neon lights,   reaching up
                  sirens flashing  to clouds
           |
         Smell
```

> Some writers prefer using a table or bullet points for their ideas. Try all the methods to see which works best for you.

> Stay focused on the title you have chosen. After planning, make sure that all your ideas and notes are focused on this title.

65

SECTION B WRITING

Had a go ☐   Nearly there ☐   Nailed it! ☐

Structure: creative

It is important to structure your creative writing effectively, and it's often best to use a narrative structure, even with descriptive writing, as you can create a vivid description by changing focus as you write.

Paper 1

5 You have been asked to submit a story to a local magazine, about returning home after being away for a long time.   **(40 marks)**

> Think for a minute about what they will be feeling and thinking. Where have they been, and what has made them come back? What kind of response do they think that they will get?

Guided

1 Which narrative viewpoint will you use? Circle two options.

   First person   or   Third person   and   Present tense   or   Past tense

2 Complete the narrative structure for your story, entitled 'Going Back'. Remember to include ideas about appropriate creative writing techniques in your plan.

Exposition: *Use the senses: what does the narrator see, hear or smell as they approach the place?*

Approaching a house – it's run-down, but can smell wood-smoke from a chimney, and hear birds – shocked by how quiet it seems to be. ....

....

Complication: .... *Use a metaphor or simile:*

....

Crisis: .... *Use dramatic adjectives or verbs:*

....

Resolution: ....

....

---

3 You can make your writing more interesting, or more tense, by playing with the narrative structure. Rewrite the plan in Question 2, but this time start at the crisis and use flashbacks to tell the story:

Crisis: ....

Exposition: ....

Complication: ....

Return to crisis: ....

Resolution: ....

Had a go ☐ Nearly there ☐ Nailed it! ☐

SECTION B WRITING

Beginnings and endings: creative

The beginning of your creative writing needs to engage the reader, immediately hooking them and setting the tone for the rest of your story or description.

Look at this exam-style question. **You don't need to answer this question now.** Instead, think about what it is asking you to do, then answer Questions 1 and 2.

Paper 1

> 5 Your school magazine is asking for examples of creative writing for next month's edition.
> Write a story about an unexpected discovery.
> **(40 marks)**

1 You will need to start with some quick planning: complete the list below to get started.

> Listing some quick ideas before you start will help you feel more confident.

One-sentence description of the storyline: ....

....

Narrative voice: .... (first/third person)

Where is the story set? ....

Who is the main character? ....

> Having these ideas in mind will help you to get started more easily.

2 There are many different styles of opening you could adopt. Look at the examples given, and write a beginning that sets a tone of conflict or danger.

> Don't overdo it with dialogue. Make sure you mainly use prose to demonstrate your sentence structure.

Dialogue	Setting the scene using the senses
'How could you do that?' my sister hissed.	Neon lights made the pavement light up like a rainbow, gleaming on the slick wet tarmac and creating pathways for the unhappy to follow.
A mystery	**Conflict or danger**
I never meant it to happen like that. When we left the house that morning, I had no idea everything was about to change.	

The ending of a piece of creative writing is just as important as the opening. Choose one of the examples from Question 2, then answer Questions 3 and 4.

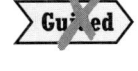

Guided

3 What will the tone of your ending be? Will it be happy, tense or sad? Write a sentence explaining how you will end your story.

....

....

Guided

4 Write three possible final sentences. Make sure you focus on using the tone you selected.

(a) ....

(b) ....

(c) ....

SECTION B WRITING

Had a go ☐   Nearly there ☐   Nailed it! ☐

Putting it into practice

Read the exam-style question below. **You don't need to answer this question**. Instead, think about the question options, then answer Questions 1 and 2.

Paper 1

5 Write a short story for submission to a writing magazine for teenagers.

Either:

Write a description suggested by this picture:

Or:

Write a short story about feeling unnoticed. **(40 marks)**

> When you plan for this type of question in the exam, remember to:
> - read each question option carefully
> - decide which question to answer
> - spend 5 minutes on a detailed plan
> - plan the narrative voice and creative writing techniques you will use.

1 Choose one of the question options from the exam-style question above. Then use the space below to plan your answer.

One-sentence description of the storyline: ....

....

Narrative voice: ....

Where is the story set? ....

Who is the main character? ....

Guided 2 Add some more planning notes here:

....

....

....

....

....

....

....

Had a go ☐   Nearly there ☐   Nailed it! ☐

SECTION B WRITING

Ideas and planning: viewpoint 1

Read the exam-style question below. **You don't need to answer this question.** Instead, think about what it is asking you to do, then answer Question 1.

Paper ②

5 'Festivals and fairs should be banned. They encourage bad behaviour and are disruptive to local communities.'

Write a letter to your MP in which you explain your point of view on this statement. **(40 marks)**

1 Plan an answer to the exam-style question. Work through the planning stages and complete the box diagram below. One example has been added for you.

   (a) Decide whether you agree or disagree with the point of view in the question. Summarise your response: ....
   ....

   (b) To guide readers, plan an introduction that tells them what you are writing and why they should read it. Add it to the diagram.

   (c) Decide on the three key points you will make.

   (d) Decide on the evidence you will use to support your key points.

   (e) Sequence your key points by numbering them. What would be the most logical or effective order?

   (f) Add a counter-argument to your plan. What might someone who opposed your opinion argue? How can you dismiss their argument?

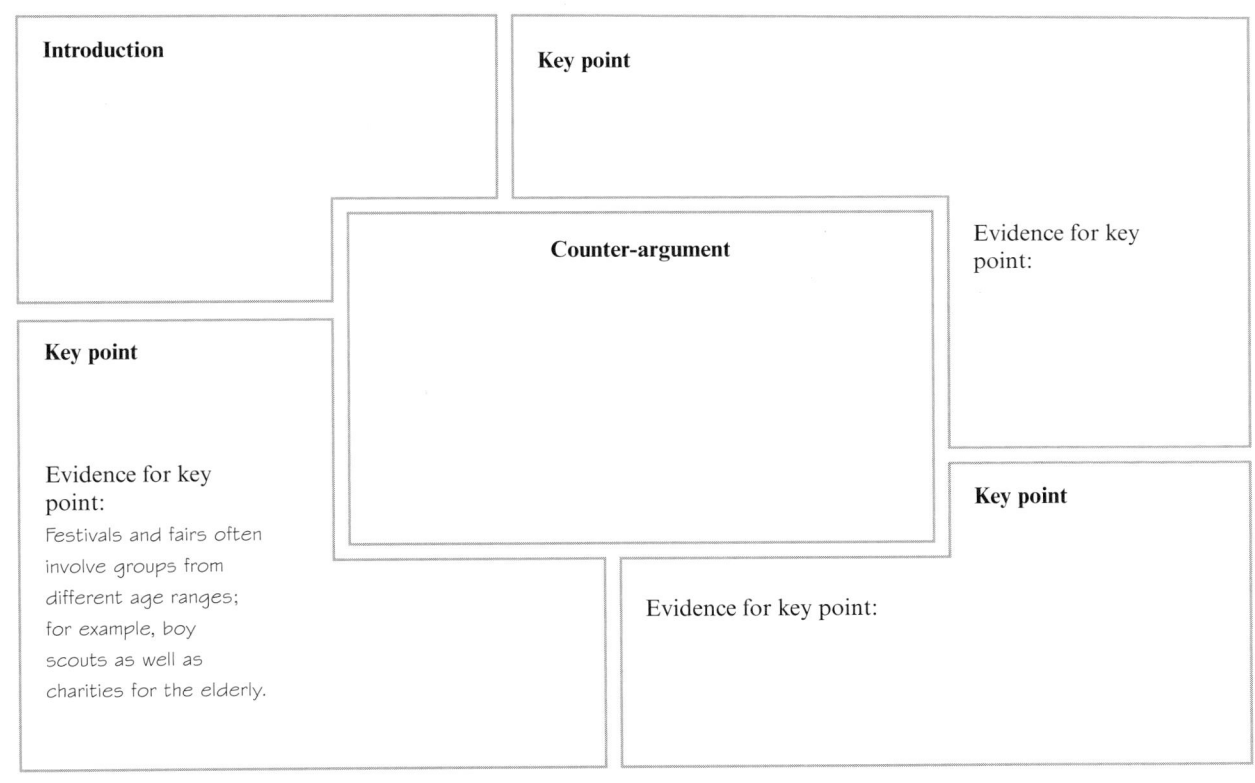

Introduction	Key point
	Counter-argument	Evidence for key point:
Key point		
Evidence for key point: *Festivals and fairs often involve groups from different age ranges; for example, boy scouts as well as charities for the elderly.*		**Key point**
		Evidence for key point:

   (g) Make some notes for a conclusion that will reinforce your point of view.
   ....
   ....
   ....
   ....

Remember:
- You only have 45 minutes to plan, write and check this task – so aim for six paragraphs of well-crafted writing.
- Quality is far more important than quantity.

SECTION B WRITING   Had a go ☐   Nearly there ☐   Nailed it! ☐

Ideas and planning: viewpoint 2

Read the exam-style question below. **You don't need to answer this question**. Instead, think about what it is asking you to do, then answer Question 1.

Paper 2

5 'Wildlife documentaries are far too graphic. We shouldn't have to watch animals killing each other to learn about nature.'

Write a report for a television channel explaining your point of view on this statement. **(40 marks)**

1 Plan an answer to the exam-style question. Work through the planning stages and complete the box diagram below. Some ideas have been added for you.
   (a) Plan your introduction. Tell your reader what you are writing about and why it is important.
   (b) You will need at least three key points. Decide which key points you will include.
   (c) Add detailed ideas to each of your key points, including techniques appropriate to your audience and purpose.
   (d) Number your key points. Which will work best at the beginning and which at the end?
   (e) Plan your conclusion.

> Add ideas for temporal adverbials that would help to guide your reader through your points. Temporal adverbials describe when the action of a verb is carried out, e.g. just the other day, last month.

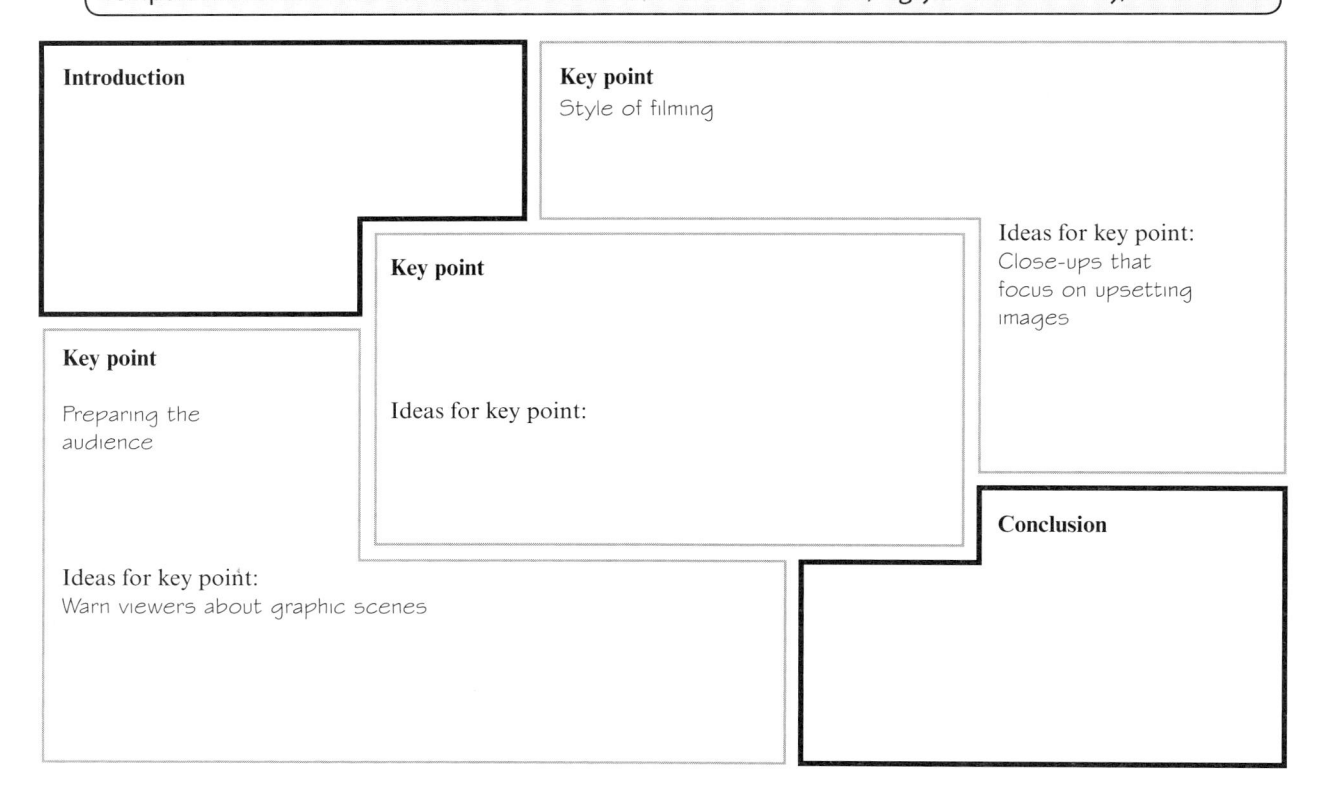

Introduction

Key point
Style of filming

Key point

Ideas for key point:

Key point
Preparing the audience

Ideas for key point:
Warn viewers about graphic scenes

Ideas for key point:
Close-ups that focus on upsetting images

Conclusion

> **Remember:** You have 45 minutes to complete your writing of this question in the exam, including 5 minutes for planning and 5 minutes for checking.

> Plan your writing carefully – quality is more important than quantity, but responses will need to be developed and sustained.

Had a go ☐   Nearly there ☐   Nailed it! ☐

SECTION B WRITING

Openings: viewpoint

Read the exam-style question below. **You don't need to answer this question now.** Instead, think about what it is asking you to do, then answer Questions 1 and 2.

Paper 2

> 5 'Alcohol is a dangerous drug and should be banned.'
>
> Write an article for a national newspaper in which you explain your point of view on this statement.
>
> **(40 marks)**

1 The first sentences of your writing must grab the reader's attention and make them want to read on. Try writing the opening sentence of your response to the exam-style question above in lots of different ways.

Using a rhetorical question: ....

....

Making a bold or controversial statement: ....

....

With a relevant quotation: ....

....

With a shocking or surprising fact or statistic: ....

....

With a short, relevant, interesting anecdote: Watching my own grandfather die as a result of alcoholism was a traumatic experience. He lost his health, his home and all sense of hope.

> Don't waste time telling the reader what you are going to write (e.g. 'In this article I am going to argue that ...'). This is not an interesting opening. Instead, hook them in with a catchy starting sentence.

Guided

2 Now write for the other viewpoint to the exam-style question. Choose two of your ideas from Question 1 and use them to write counter-arguments.

....
....
....
....
....
....
....

> To deal with opposing ideas, use words like 'however', 'on the other hand' or 'nevertheless'.

SECTION B WRITING

Had a go ☐   Nearly there ☐   Nailed it! ☐

Conclusions: viewpoint

Read the exam-style question below. **You don't need to answer this question now.** Instead, think about what it is asking you to do, then answer Questions 1 and 2.

Paper 2

5 'Alcohol is a dangerous drug and should be banned.'

Write an article for a national newspaper in which you explain your point of view on this statement.

(40 marks)

Guided 1 Match the examples of conclusions to their correct description.

(a) If society doesn't tackle the scourge of alcohol, future generations will pay the price.

Vivid image

(b) The government must do more to tackle this terrible disease; it is time for this country to go dry once and for all.

Warning

(c) A red-eyed man sits alone at the bar, hands shaking and staring into the bottom of an empty glass. Don't let that be you.

Happy note

(d) How can we allow people to consume something that causes untold damage to their health?

'Call to action'

(e) Young people can misbehave when intoxicated but, in most cases, they learn to control themselves. We all grow up eventually.

Thought-provoking question

Guided 2 Choose an example from Question 1 and write two good points about it. Then write your own version of this style of ending.

Type of example: ....

Good point 1: ....

Good point 2: ....

My version: ....

....

....

....

....

> A conclusion should summarise all the points made in your writing to round off your argument on a memorable note with a clear understanding of your views. Don't forget to refer to your introduction when writing your conclusion.

Had a go ☐ Nearly there ☐ Nailed it! ☐

SECTION B WRITING

Putting it into practice

Guided

Read the exam-style question below. **You don't need to answer this question**. Instead, think about what you are being asked to do, then answer Question 1.

Paper 2

> 5 'A law should be put in place that requires all 16-year-olds to do community service.'
>
> Write a letter to a national newspaper in which you argue for or against this statement.
>
> **(40 marks)**

> When you plan for this type of question in the exam, remember to:
> - read the question carefully and identify the topic
> - identify the form, audience and purpose before you start
> - spend 5 minutes planning your answer
> - note down the features and techniques you will use to support the form, audience and purpose
> - organise and sequence your ideas
> - plan your introduction and conclusion.

1 Use the space below to plan your answer to the exam-style question above. Use a spider diagram to organise your ideas.

SECTION B WRITING

Had a go ☐ Nearly there ☐ Nailed it! ☐

Paragraphing

Look at this exam-style question.

> **Paper 2**
>
> 5 'Pupils should be allowed to choose where they want to sit in lessons.'
>
> Write an article for your school magazine in which you explain your point of view on this statement.
>
> **(40 marks)**

Read this student's response to the exam-style question, then answer Questions 1 to 4.

> Giving pupils the choice of where they sit may sound like a good idea but it would cause confusion and disagreements. What would happen if ten students all decided they wanted to sit at a table designed for four people? The teacher is the professional in the room and is paid to make sensible judgements about where individuals ought to be placed. Children are not mature enough to make these decisions. Seating plans may not be popular but they are there for very good reasons.

This student has organised the paragraphs in her argument using **Point–Evidence–Explain**.

Guided 1 Identify and annotate the answer showing the three different sections: point, evidence and explain.

2 A student has written down some ideas in response to this exam style question. Identify which are **points**, which are **evidence**, and which are **explanation**.

(a) People concentrate less on class and more on talking. ....

(b) Test scores were 10% lower when pupils were distracted. ....

(c) Boys are more likely to distract other pupils. ....

(d) Girls might feel uncomfortable being made to sit at a table with boys. ....

(e) I work better sitting next to the people I like. ....

(f) It is fun to sit by your friends but that is not good for learning. ....

(g) People are more likely to ask friends questions. ....

(h) Less worry of looking foolish. ....

(i) Some students work better when seated with quiet pupils. ....

Guided 3 Now choose a point, evidence and explanation from Question 2 to write your own answer.

....

....

....

....

....

....

....

Guided 4 Identify and label the three different sections of your paragraph: **point**, **evidence** and **explain**.

> For each new point you make, start a new paragraph. When writing to inform, explain or describe, start each paragraph with a topic sentence (a sentence that expresses the main idea of the paragraph).

Had a go ☐   Nearly there ☐   Nailed it! ☐

SECTION B WRITING

Linking ideas

Different adverbs and adverbial phrases have different purposes.

1 Copy the adverbs (or adverbial phrases) listed into the table, adding each one to the correct column.

Consequently	Additionally	In particular	Importantly
For example	Nevertheless	In the same way	Equally
For instance	Alternatively	Moreover	Therefore

Adding an idea	Explaining	Illustrating	Emphasising	Comparing	Contrasting
		For example	Importantly		

> Your argument will be stronger if you use adverbials to link your points together.

Read the exam-style question below. **You don't need to answer this question now.** Instead, think about what it is asking you to do, then answer Questions 2 and 3.

Paper 2

5 'Festivals and fairs should be banned. They encourage bad behaviour and are disruptive to local communities.'

Write a letter to your MP in which you explain your point of view on this statement. **(40 marks)**

Guided

2 Look at the paragraphs below. They are extracts from one student's response to the exam-style question above. Fill in all of the gaps using appropriate adverbials.

> Fairs and festivals appeal to each generation and are used to mark special occasions. ...., we should recognise the role they play in bringing the community together. Young and old can let down their hair and .... we should ignore calls for these glorious events to be outlawed by miserable individuals.

> Of course, there are some downsides to fairs and festivals, ... an increase in noise and litter. ...., I believe that this is a small price to pay for the undoubted positives associated with these joyful celebrations.

Guided

3 Now write your own Point–Evidence–Explain paragraph in response to the exam-style question above. Remember to use a range of adverbials to guide the reader through your argument.

....
....
....
....
....
....
....

> Remember to start with a topic sentence. Re-reading the planning you did on page 69 will help you.

SECTION B WRITING

Had a go ☐ Nearly there ☐ Nailed it! ☐

Putting it into practice

Answer the exam-style question below. Focus in particular on your use of paragraphs and adverbials.

5 'Graffiti is ugly and makes the local area look scruffy. Anyone caught doing it should be harshly punished.'

Write a report to your local council in which you argue for or against this statement. **(40 marks)**

> When you tackle any writing question in the exam, remember to:
> - write in paragraphs
> - plan one main point or idea per paragraph
> - use P–E–E to structure your paragraphs
> - organise and sequence your paragraphs
> - use adverbials to link your paragraphs and guide your reader through your ideas.

> **Remember**: You have more space than this to answer your question in the exam. Use your own paper to finish your answer to the question above.

Had a go ☐   Nearly there ☐   Nailed it! ☐

SECTION B WRITING

Formality and standard English 1

1 Match each phrase to the situation where its register would be appropriate. One answer has been completed for you.

- A: Her outfit is so on point.
- B: Aren't we old enough to make our own decisions?
- C: Could you please pass me that?
- D: Looking at the statistics for the last eight years ...

Conversation with friend   Conversation with stranger   Speech to scientists   Speech to peers

- E: Everyone hates wearing school uniform.
- F: It is a pleasure to meet you.
- G: That was an epic fail.
- H: It is true that this is not the most popular opinion.

> **Standard English** is very formal. **Colloquial language** is informal but not rude.
> **Slang** is very informal and can be rude. **Register** is language used for a specific purpose or setting.

Read the exam-style question and then look at the example student answer below.

Paper 2

5 'Nurses should be paid the same as Members of Parliament.'
Write a letter to your MP in which you explain your point of view on this statement. **(40 marks)**

> To Dave,
>
> It's okay for you, wearing fancy suits and living in a posh house. What about poor nurses busting there guts for next to nothing? Just because your rolling in it doesn't mean the rest of us aren't screwed. It's just not right. Me mum says your all bloody useless and only look out for yourselves. You need 2 sort it out.

2 (a) Annotate the answer with advice you might give the student, based on their opening paragraph.

(b) Rewrite the paragraph in standard English, ensuring that the writing is matched to the purpose and audience.

> You should avoid using slang when writing formally.
>
> Avoid the common mistake of mixing up the homophones 'there', 'their' and 'they're' and 'your' and 'you're'.

Dear Mr Smith,

I would like to draw your attention to the issue of nurses' pay ....

....

....

Guided

3 Your friend has asked you for help. He has been asked to write a tweet for the school magazine's Twitter account to promote their new article on getting enough sleep, but cannot fit it into 140 characters. What advice would you give him to rewrite it?

My dear colleagues. Would you mind giving me a few moments of your time to reflect on

my long list of ideas for how you might get more sleep? If so, then please take the time to

peruse the latest issue of our school magazine.

....

....

77

SECTION B WRITING

Had a go ☐   Nearly there ☐   Nailed it! ☐

Formality and standard English 2

Look at the two exam-style questions below, then answer Questions 1 and 2.

Paper A (2)

5 'Skate parks are noisy places that encourage dangerous behaviour.'
Write a letter to the chair of governors of your school in which you explain your point of view on this statement.   **(40 marks)**

Paper B (2)

5 'Skate parks are noisy places that encourage dangerous behaviour.'
Write an article for a teenage skating website in which you explain your point of view on this statement.   **(40 marks)**

Guided

1 Look at the sentences below. Which exam question would their tone be appropriate for? Label each sentence 'Paper A', 'Paper B' or 'Both'.

> Think about the audience you are aiming at. For example, would you be less interested in an article if it started 'My dear reader...'?

Point of view: first or third person

| Many adults believe that skate parks encourage anti-social behaviour and cause nasty injuries. | I believe that skate parks are safe places for young people to have some harmless fun. |

Standard English or non-standard English

| Why do some people have an issue with young people having fun and enjoyment in their lives? | Kids ain't bothering anybody, man. They just wanna chill out and blow off some steam. |

2 Rewrite the following student answer using more formal language.

> Everything us kids do seems to rub the oldies up the wrong way. It's time they thought about the next generation for a change. Why can't they see that skate parks are brill places to hang out? Chill out grandpa!

> Think about using more complicated words and phrases, replacing slang or informal expressions, using lists, using adverbials and keeping your style emotionless.

It would appear that everything young people do nowadays is a source of irritation for the older generation. ....

....

....

....

....

> Carefully consider your audience before you start writing. Formal and informal language, standard English, slang, humour and point of view can all affect the tone of your writing.

Had a go ☐   Nearly there ☐   Nailed it! ☐

SECTION B WRITING

Vocabulary for effect: synonyms

Synonyms are words with similar meanings. For example, synonyms for 'change' include 'alteration' or 'transformation'. You can use them to avoid repetition and to add variety to your writing.

1 Look at the sentence below. Think of **at least two** synonyms for each circled word and use them to rewrite the sentence. Some examples are given below.

> Remember – good vocabulary is important, but don't use words when you're uncertain of their meaning, and be selective in your language.

(Everyone) (stared) at me in (shock) like I was (crazy).

The crowd gazed at me in fright like I was ....
.... at me in .... like I was ....
.... at me in .... like I was ....

> Some words have slightly different connotations, even if they have similar meanings. For example, 'shocking' someone is not the always the same as 'frightening' them.

2 Look at each of the words in the table below. Complete the table by adding at least two synonyms for each word. An example has been done for you.

tired	run	big	tiptoed	laugh
exhausted weary				

Look at the exam-style question below. Think about what you might include in a response to this question, then answer Question 3.

Paper 1

5 Write the opening part of a story about an embarrassing moment. **(40 marks)**

3 Write a paragraph in response to the exam-style question above. Use some of your vocabulary from Question 2 in your writing and make it as dramatic as possible.

Looking back, it was the worst moment I'd ever experienced. I wasn't alone either. I was with
....
....
....

Guided

4 Now rewrite your response to the exam-style question above. This time, choose synonyms that make it seem as uninteresting as possible.

....
....
....
....
....

SECTION B WRITING

Had a go ☐   Nearly there ☐   Nailed it! ☐

Vocabulary for effect: creative

1. Look at this description.

   > The dog standing in front of me was really big. It was also white. It looked angry. It was standing on some brown grass that was quite long.

   Rewrite the above sentence to show the scene, rather than simply telling the reader what is happening. An example has been started for you.

   The monstrous beast was standing before me ....

   ....

   ....

   ....

   > Instead of describing it as a whole, try focusing on the parts of the dog that matter. If you were facing it, what would you notice? Use actions and description to show the important points. The dog baring its teeth is more interesting than saying it looks angry.

Guided

2. Look again at your answer to Question 1. Did you focus more on the dog or on the grass it was standing on? Write a sentence explaining why.

   ....

   ....

   ....

Look at the exam-style question below, then answer Question 3.

Paper 1

5. Your entry will be judged by journalists.
   Describe somewhere you remember vividly.

   (40 marks)

Guided

3. A student's answer has been included below. Cross out where you think there is too much description, and underline where you think it could be written more effectively.

   > Remember to think about what you learned about on page 65 – setting the scene through the senses.

   > The rich sugar-sweet and strong smell of the pink, blue, purple, orange and red flowers, which danced randomly and illogically in the wind blowing, the boiling warmth from the sun heating everything below it and the loud continuous sound of the crickets making a lot of noise. I could see the beach and the sea. The food was delicious. If I close my eyes I can pretend I am still there.

Guided

4. Look at the parts you have underlined in Question 3. Pick one or two of them to rewrite below.

   ....

   ....

   ....

   ....

   ....

   ....

Had a go ☐   Nearly there ☐   Nailed it! ☐

SECTION B WRITING

Vocabulary for effect: viewpoint

Emotive words are important when you are writing to argue or persuade.

1 Look at the sentences below. Rewrite them, using emotive language to add more impact.

(a) Salaries are too low to pay for food and shelter.

   On current salaries, people are forced to starve and live on the streets.

(b) Litter takes many years to biodegrade.

   Rubbish dumped ....

   ....

(c) Going to bed late will make you tired.

   Refusing to ....

   ....

Guided

2 Look at this sentence:

   Some might argue that the (discussion) about this issue is over-rated.

   What would be the impact of replacing the circled word with 'misery', 'depression' or 'concern'?

   misery: ....

   ....

   depression: ....

   ....

   concern: ....

   ....

   For more practice with synonyms, look at page 79.

Look at the exam-style question below. **You don't need to answer this question now.** Instead, think about what you might include in a response to this question, then answer Question 3.

Paper 2

5 'Technology today has taken over our lives. People need to relax more.'

   Write an article for a magazine in which you explain your point of view on this statement.

   (40 marks)

3 Write two or three sentences in response to the exam-style question above. Aim to choose vocabulary for its impact and its connotations.

   Technology consumes every ....

   ....

   ....

   ....

   ....

SECTION B WRITING

Had a go ☐   Nearly there ☐   Nailed it! ☐

Language for different effects 1

You can add power and impact to your writing by using a range of language techniques.

1 Look at the extracts from students' writing below. Some are taken from a piece of creative writing, some from a piece of writing presenting a viewpoint. Connect the rhetorical devices to the extracts. There might be more than one answer per technique.

A: What could he possibly mean?

B: All around me, there was confusion: people running with pushchairs, screaming toddlers, the ice-cream truck pulling up its sign.

C: How could he have believed it was possible?

Rhetorical question

Contrast

Repetition

List

D: The filth and waste receded as the clean, clear water of the ocean came in.

E: The one possibility – the only possibility – was that we should take it with us.

F: Where the smallest thrill of light exists, no darkness can be found.

> A rhetorical question will end in a question mark.

Now look at the exam-style question below. **You don't need to answer this question now.** Instead, think about the language techniques you might use in a response, then answer Question 2.

Paper 2

5 'If teenagers are old enough to drive, then they are old enough to vote.'

Write an article for your local newspaper in which you argue for or against this statement.

(40 marks)

2 Use some or all of the language techniques explored in Question 1 to write four extracts which could be used in an answer to the exam-style question above.

(a) What qualifies ....

....

....

(b) Voting, like driving, needs ....

....

....

(c) ....

....

....

(d) ....

....

....

Language for different effects 2

Had a go ☐   Nearly there ☐   Nailed it! ☐

SECTION B WRITING

You can add power and impact to your writing by using a range of language techniques.

1. Here are three example sentences. Rewrite each one using direct address, pattern of three and alliteration. An example has been done for you.

   Many people drop litter.

   Direct address: Don't drop your crisp packet and pretend that it will magically go away!
   Pattern of three: ....
   Alliteration: ....

   > Don't forget that direct address can also be a rhetorical question.

   Some people play music loudly even late at night.

   Direct address: ....
   Pattern of three: ....
   Alliteration: ....

   Flying can be an uncomfortable experience.

   Direct address: ....
   Pattern of three: ....
   Alliteration: ....

2. Now look at this example sentence. Rewrite it three times using hyperbole, making each more exaggerated than the last. One has been completed for you.

   The person sat in front of me talked loudly on their mobile phone.

   (a) The rude person boomed into their mobile phone as loud as a speaker.
   (b) ....
   ....
   (c) ....
   ....

Guided 3. Look back at your answers to Question 2. Which do you think is the most effective and why?

   ....
   ....
   ....
   ....
   ....

SECTION B WRITING

Had a go ☐   Nearly there ☐   Nailed it! ☐

Language for different effects 3

Figurative language can be used to create powerful images in the mind of a reader.

1. Look at the examples of figurative language used in the sentences below. The writers have used similes, metaphors and personification to give their writing impact. But which sentence uses which technique? Circle the correct answer. One has been completed for you.

> A **simile** compares one thing to another, often using 'like' or 'as'.
> A **metaphor** says one thing *is* another to create comparison.
> **Personification** gives non-human objects human characteristics.

A	The wind whistled a sombre tune	Simile	Metaphor	Personification
B	The road to success was blocked by walls of disappointment.	Simile	Metaphor	Personification
C	She grinned like an evil clown.	(Simile)	Metaphor	Personification
D	Waiting for Dad to make dinner, I feel like a bear coming out of hibernation.	Simile	Metaphor	Personification
E	The man was cruel. He had a heart of stone.	Simile	Metaphor	Personification
F	My homework stared at me from the desk. 'You better finish me at some point,' its look suggested.	Simile	Metaphor	Personification

Now look at the exam-style question below. **You don't need to answer this question now.** Instead, think about the figurative language you might use in a response, then answer Question 2.

Paper 2

5. 'Play areas in parks should only be used by under-14s.'
   Write a letter to the local council arguing for or against this statement. **(40 marks)**

2. Write four sentences that might appear in an answer to the exam-style question above. Use one of the figurative devices explored in Question 1 in each sentence.

   Simile: It is as clear as ....

   ....

   Metaphor: Children are imprisoned by ....

   ....

   Personification: ....

   ....

   Simile and personification: Older teenagers are noisy as ....

   ....

Had a go ☐   Nearly there ☐   Nailed it! ☐

SECTION B WRITING

Putting it into practice

Write a response to the exam-style question below. Focus in particular on your use of language and language techniques for effect.

5 A creative writing website aimed at teenagers is having a competition.

Either:

Write the opening of a story inspired by this image.

Or:

Write a story about discovering a key.   **(40 marks)**

....
....
....
....
....
....
....
....
....
....
....
....
....
....
....
....
....

Remember: You have more space than this to answer your question in the exam. Use your own paper to finish your answer to the question above.

SECTION B WRITING

Had a go ☐ Nearly there ☐ Nailed it! ☐

Putting it into practice

Guided

Answer the exam-style question below. Focus in particular on your use of language and language techniques to present a viewpoint.

Paper 2

5 'Young people's local facilities deserve to have money spent on them.'

Write a letter to your MP in which you explain your point of view on this statement. **(40 marks)**

> When you tackle any writing question in the exam, you should think about language.
> Remember to:
> - annotate the question to highlight the form, audience and purpose
> - choose language that is appropriate for the audience and purpose
> - choose language techniques with care and for impact
> - avoid using too many techniques – it is more important that your writing is well structured and appropriate for the audience and purpose.

Remember: You have more space than this to answer your question in the exam. Use your own paper to finish your answer to the question above.

Had a go ☐   Nearly there ☐   Nailed it! ☐

SECTION B WRITING

Sentence variety 1

Using a range of different sentence types adds variety to your writing and helps to convey your ideas clearly and to engage your reader.

1. Look at the sentences (a – e) and identify the sentence type from the list (A – E). Then write a sentence to explain how you know. Two have been done for you.

   A   a single-clause sentence

   B   a multi-clause sentence with a subordinate clause

   C   a multi-clause sentence with a coordinate clause

   D   a multi-clause sentence with a relative clause

   E   a minor sentence

   (a) The castle, which had previously stood for years, had disappeared overnight.

   Type: ....
   Explanation: ....

   (b) No way!

   Type E
   Explanation: It has no verb.

   (c) I tried, but nothing worked.

   Type: ....
   Explanation: ....

   (d) If we don't leave, then everything will change.

   Type: ....
   Explanation: ....

   (e) It was always like this.

   Type: ....
   Explanation: It has only one clause, with just one verb.

Look at the exam-style question below. **You don't need to answer this question now**. First, think how you might use different sentence types in a response.

Paper 2

5   'People who work for their local community are the real heroes of today.'

Write a lively article for a newspaper arguing either for or against this statement.   **(40 marks)**

Now consider this extract from one student's answer to the exam-style question above, then answer Question 2.

> Firefighters, police officers and local charity workers are all heroes as they work tirelessly every day for other people and putting themselves at risk is a daily occurrence for them so comparing them with celebrity role models is a joke because there is no comparison to the real work they do alongside a celebrity who is only famous for looking attractive or kicking a ball around.

2. The extract from the student's answer is just one long sentence. Rewrite the extract. Aim to use a variety of at least three different sentence types.

   Firefighters, police offers and local charity workers ....
   ....
   ....

   > Remember, the best answers use a variety of long and short sentences.

SECTION B WRITING

Had a go ☐   Nearly there ☐   Nailed it! ☐

Sentence variety 2

Look at the exam-style question below. **You don't need to answer this question now.** Instead, think about what you might include in a response, then answer Questions 1 and 2.

Paper 1

5 A magazine is running a writing competition that will be judged by students your own age. Write the opening of a story about uncertainty.

(40 marks)

A student has written their response to the exam-style question.

> Initially, I was really unsure about starting a new school. Naturally, I found it hard to get out of bed. Unfortunately, it was next to a scary-looking factory. Scarily, it all turned out to be a nightmare. Frustratingly, I couldn't remember anyone's name or where anything was. Eventually, though, I managed to make a friend. Sadly, she moved away soon after.

Guided

1 What type of opener have they used for every sentence? ....

2 Choose three of their sentences and rewrite them using different openers. One has been done for you.

I really did not want to leave the safety of my warm and comfy bed.

....

....

> The seven types of sentence opener are:
> - a pronoun (I, he, she, they)
> - an article (a, an, the)
> - a preposition (below, next to)
> - an –ing word (or present participle) (thinking, sighing)
> - an adjective (sad, dark)
> - an adverb (wobbly, sulkily)
> - a conjunction (if, because).

3 Now write your own paragraph in response to the above exam-style question. Aim to use:
   - all seven different types of sentence opener in your writing
   - a different word to start each of your sentences.

> Choose the first word of each sentence carefully. Varying the first word can make your writing more interesting.

Although I was usually ....

....

....

....

....

....

....

> It is easy to accidentally start a lot of sentences with 'The' or 'I', but this can make your writing sound repetitive.

Had a go ☐   Nearly there ☐   Nailed it! ☐

SECTION B WRITING

Sentences for different effects

Read the example text.

> The boy hit the kerb, fell off his bike, went flying over the handlebars, skidded across the concrete, shredded his bloodied knees, before coming to a halt. The silence was brief.

Guided

1. In the example above, a **long sentence** is followed by a **short sentence**. What effect is this intended to have on the reader?

   Think about the different pace or tone at the end.

   ....
   ....

2. In the sentences below the same ideas have been used, but in a different order.

   > A Before I asked Dad for permission to go to the party, I polished his beloved car until it gleamed in the late evening sunlight, while he watched from the window with a quizzical expression.

   > B While he watched from the window with a quizzical expression, I polished dad's beloved car until it gleamed in the late evening sunlight before asking him for permission to go to the party.

   How does the order in which the information is organised affect each sentence's emphasis?

   The first sentence in text A emphasises ....
   ....
   ....

Look at the exam-style question below. **You don't need to answer this question now.** Instead, think about how you might begin an answer, then answer Question 3.

Paper 2

5. 'Recycling your household waste isn't worth the effort. It makes no difference while factories are still pumping out pollution.'

   Write a speech for a Year 11 assembly arguing either for or against this statement. **(40 marks)**

   Make sure you don't put too much information into one sentence that is spread over a number of subordinate clauses. If you do this, the reader will lose interest in your argument.

3. Write the opening two or three sentences of your own response to the exam-style question above. Aim to include:
   - a long sentence followed by a short sentence
   - a sentence structured to give specific emphasis.

   Recently, I watched all my neighbours lug brown bins to the end of their drives. As I walked past, I thought ....
   ....
   ....
   ....

SECTION B WRITING

Had a go ☐   Nearly there ☐   Nailed it! ☐

Putting it into practice

Guided — Answer the exam-style question below. Focus in particular on varying your sentences for effect.

Paper 2

5 'Children who choose to work should expect to be paid less than an adult for the same job.'

Write an article for a national newspaper in which you explain your point of view on this statement.

(40 marks)

> When you tackle any writing question in the exam, you should think about sentence variety. Remember to:
> - use a range of sentence types
> - start your sentences in a range of different ways
> - structure your sentences for effect
> - avoid overloading individual sentences with too much information.

> **Remember**: You have more space than this to answer your question in the exam. Use your own paper to finish your answer to the question above.

Had a go ☐   Nearly there ☐   Nailed it! ☐

SECTION B WRITING

Ending a sentence

Failing to use full stops, question marks, exclamation marks and capital letters correctly affects the quality of your writing.

Guided 1 Write in the punctuation you should use to end each sentence.

(a) The bike was rusty and its paint had chipped off

(b) What do you mean you couldn't find the monkey

(c) I never really liked him

(d) Have you never seen a thousand pounds before

(e) Stop or you'll crash

> Remember to use a full stop at the end of a statement, an exclamation mark at the end of an exclamation and a question mark at the end of a question. 'That's what he said!', 'That's what he said.' and 'That's what he said?' have quite different meanings.

2 Write a sentence using each type of ending punctuation. The first one has been done for you.

(a) Full stop: The wind blew him over three times before he finally got home.

(b) Question mark: ....

(c) Exclamation mark: ....

Guided 3 Look at the sentences below.

(a) Tick the two sentences that are punctuated correctly. Cross out the one that is not.

A   Cycle helmets can save lives, I never ride my bike without wearing one.

B   Cycle helmets can save lives. I never ride my bike without wearing one.

C   Cycle helmets can save lives so I never ride my bike without wearing one.

> It is incorrect to use a comma to join two complete clauses in a sentence. Use a full stop to separate them or join them using a conjunction. You'll need to check every time you use a comma. Ask yourself – does it need a comma or is the sentence complete?

(b) Now explain your decision.

....

4 Annotate this student's writing, correcting all the full stop, question mark and exclamation mark errors you can find. One error has been underlined for you.

> The Cave of Doom!!!
>
> I stumbled towards the gloomy cave, fear gripped me with its icy fingers and ran a fearful shiver down my spine. My skin began to crawl and sweat erupted around my forehead. What was this horrible place. Could I bring myself to enter the mouth of hell?.
>
> Turning back was not an option, I had come this far and must enter this hateful hole. I held my nerve, my head was spinning and my legs felt like they belonged to a different being. I called out in fear, my words echoed across the darkness, it was like listening to a large demonic creature.

SECTION B WRITING

Had a go ☐ Nearly there ☐ Nailed it! ☐

Commas

If you are confident with using commas, you will write more effective multi-clause sentences and lists.

1 Look at the sentences below. Some have used commas correctly. Some have not. Tick the correct sentences and cross the incorrect ones. One has been done for you.

Commas in lists

☒ A My favourite meal, is cheeseburger and chips or spaghetti Bolognese.

☐ B The most popular pizza toppings include cheese, ham, mushrooms, sweetcorn, pineapple and peppers.

☐ C To clean a kitchen properly you will need a mop, bucket, cloth, disinfectant and plenty of elbow grease.

Commas in multi-clause sentences with subordinate clauses

☐ D Whether we enjoy them or not, vegetables should be a central part of our diet.

☐ E Vegetables should be a part of our diet whether we enjoy eating them or not.

☐ F After working in a sausage factory my father never ate sausages again.

Commas in multi-clause sentences with relative clauses

☐ G The potato which is a good source of energy, should not count towards your five-a-day.

☐ H Asparagus traditionally eaten with the fingers is in season from April to June.

☐ I My kitchen knife, which was made by Japanese craftsmen, is extremely sharp.

Guided 2 Look again at all the sentences in Question 1. Annotate the sentences to correct any that you marked as incorrect.

Look at the exam-style question below. **You don't need to answer this question now.** Instead, think about what you might include in a response, then answer Question 3.

Paper 1

5 Write a story which involves a family meal. **(40 marks)**

3 Write three sentences in response to the exam-style question above. Use commas differently in each sentence, to separate:
- items in a list
- a main and subordinate clause
- a main and relative clause.

An example has been done for you.

> Avoid comma splices (when you use a comma instead of a full stop or conjunction to join two pieces of information in a sentence).

Before the Smith family sat down for dinner, there were the usual arguments about homework.

....
....
....
....
....
....
....

Had a go ☐   Nearly there ☐   Nailed it! ☐

SECTION B WRITING

Apostrophes and speech punctuation

Make sure you know how to avoid the common errors of missing out or using incorrect apostrophes and speech punctuation.

1 Look at the sentences below. Some have used punctuation correctly. Some have not. Tick the correct sentences and cross out the incorrect ones.

> Remember:
> - apostrophes in contractions are used to replace missing letters
> - apostrophes of possession are always placed at the end of the noun whether it's plural (girls') or singular (girl's)
> - in dialogue, there is always a punctuation mark before the closing speech marks.

Apostrophes in contractions

- [✗] A I do'nt understand how it happened.
- [ ] B John didn't get to work on time.
- [ ] C I wouldnt do that if I were you.

Apostrophes of possession

- [ ] D My dads' mobile is broken.
- [ ] E The team's improvement was unbelievable.
- [ ] F The girls' test scores were all impressive.

Speech punctuation

- [ ] G 'Give it to me!' he demanded.
- [ ] H 'It's not a problem.'
- [ ] I 'I'll get you for this.' she hissed.

Guided 2 Look again at all the sentences in Question 1. Annotate the sentences, correcting any that you marked as incorrect.

Guided 3 Now read this conversation between two parents in which they argue about whether to allow their son to go to a party at the weekend. Annotate to add the missing apostrophes and speech marks.

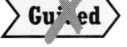

> So, she began. Dont you think its a bad idea?
>
> Arent any adults going to be there? he asked.
>
> Of course there wont be! She sighed, pulling her necklace where it had tangled in its chain.
>
> He thought about it for a moment. I dont see any problem with him going. Its not all night.
>
> Dont you remember what happened last time? she pointed out. Dont you remember the broken window?
>
> Yes, he admitted, but shrugged his shoulders like he didnt see its relevance. That was all of the students fault, not just his.
>
> Or that his bed ended up in his best friends pond?
>
> He couldn't argue about that. His sons bed hadnt been easy to fish out of Sams pond.

SECTION B WRITING

Had a go ☐   Nearly there ☐   Nailed it! ☐

Colons, semi-colons, dashes, brackets and ellipses

Punctuation helps you to express yourself clearly. It can also help you to develop your ideas.

Guided

1. Which piece of punctuation can you use on its own or in pairs? ....

   > Remember, brackets can **only** be used in pairs.

2. Look at the sentences below. In each of them an ellipsis, a semicolon, a colon or a dash has been used incorrectly, or could be replaced by other punctuation instead. Correct the sentences.

   (a) To everyone's surprise; the magician had completely vanished...

   To everyone's surprise, the magician had completely vanished.

   (b) A healthy diet is vital ... it can allow you to gain an edge over competitors – who don't take care of their bodies.

   ....

   (c) Learning to be a good loser is: essential. Everybody tastes defeat at some point.

   ....

   (d) I have always been good at the flute ... (since I can remember anyway) ... but wanted to be better.

   ....

   (e) Some cyclists take to the road; without wearing a safety helmet ... not a good idea.

   ....

   > You can use a semi-colon to link two connected ideas instead of using a conjunction.
   > You can use a colon to introduce a list, an example or an explanation
   > You only need to use three dots to show an ellipsis ...

Look at the exam-style question below. **You don't need to answer this question now.** Instead, think about what you might include in a response, then answer Question 3.

Paper 1

5. Write about a time when you lost something valuable.   **(40 marks)**

Guided

3. A student has written a response to the exam-style question, but has used some of their brackets incorrectly. Correct their answer and suggest alternative punctuation where needed.

   > Using brackets does not mean you should add irrelevant information into your description.

   > I had left no stone unturned; the precious (keepsake) was nowhere to be found. Vividly, I remember the day my grandmother (on my father's side of the family gave me this priceless family heirloom. For hours, I had scoured every corner of my bedroom (even looking down the back of the dusty cupboards – but it still remained elusive. There was now only one place where it might be: (inside the bathroom). Desperately, I rummaged through the washing basket (and searched under the cistern). The only other possible location (– unless it had been taken in the night by the tooth fairy –) was the u-bend of the sink. I unscrewed the pipe, dragged out (clumps of mildewed hair and began to sift through the filth, looking for the glint of a diamond earring ...

Had a go ☐   Nearly there ☐   Nailed it! ☐

SECTION B WRITING

Putting it into practice

Answer one of the exam-style questions below. Focus in particular on punctuation.

Paper 1

5 Write a description suggested by this picture.

(40 marks)

Paper 2

5 'Rugby is too dangerous and should become a non-contact sport.'
Write an article for a sports magazine arguing for or against this statement. **(40 marks)**

> When answering any writing question in the exam, think carefully about punctuation. Remember to:
> - use a range of punctuation accurately, including advanced punctuation such as colons and semi-colons
> - draw the symbols on your paper ; : ( ) … ' ! ? -, – and tick them off as you use them
> - plan your time carefully so that you have time to check the accuracy of your punctuation.

....
....
....
....
....
....

Remember: You have more space than this to answer your question in the exam. Use your own paper to finish your answer to the question above.

Common spelling errors 1

Some of the most common spelling errors in students' writing are a result of misusing or confusing the following:

would of and would have should of and should have could of and could have	• 'have' is correct • this mistake occurs because people say 'would've', omitting the 'have', which makes it sound like 'would of'
our and are	• 'our' – belongs to us, e.g. 'That's our house' • 'are' – auxiliary verb used to form plural present progressive tense, e.g. 'we are looking', a continuous present action
their, there and they're	• 'their' – belongs to them • 'there' – over there, position • 'they're' – they are
affect and effect	• 'affect' is usually a verb, meaning 'to make a difference to' • 'effect' is usually a noun, meaning 'the result of something' • one way to remember this can be to think of Affect being a cAuse, and Effect being a rEsult.
Words ending in -ley and -ly	• the most common ending is -ly; it's used when creating an adverb • terrible – terribly • slow – slowly • beautiful – beautifully
its and it's	• 'it's' always means 'it is' • 'its' means 'belonging to it'

1 Identify and correct any spelling errors in these sentences. The first one has been done for you.

(a) They went all the way back to there house. **their**

(b) It was too soon to know what the affect would be on him. ....

(c) Its not every day that you get to see one of those! ....

(d) He was not they're to help with there needs. ....

(e) She saw what it's problem was immediately. ....

(f) Their was nothing that would effect the problem. ....

(g) It was absolutley and scariley out of control. ....

(h) They're was a large hill that woodn't of been easy to cross. ....

(i) 'Its bad,' he said negativley, 'they know where we our hiding.' ....

(j) 'You shouldn't of said that its true!' ....

(k) We just hoped that are plan would have some affect. ....

(l) Many students felt it had effected them negativley. ....

(m) Its not the first time this has happened. ....

Guided **2** Now write a sentence about going on a journey, correctly using as many of these words as possible.

....

....

Had a go ☐   Nearly there ☐   Nailed it! ☐

SECTION B WRITING

Common spelling errors 2

Some of the most common spelling errors in students' writing are a result of misusing or confusing the following words.

your and you're	• 'your' is a pronoun, used to address someone directly • 'you're' means 'you are'
two, too and to	• 'two' – the number, e.g. 'two things you need' • 'too' – excessively or also, e.g. 'she saw things too', 'that was too much' • 'to' – preposition showing relationship of time or place, e.g. 'I went to the park', 'It is going to rain'
we're, were, where and wear	• 'we're' – we are • 'were' – past tense, e.g. 'we were singing' • 'where' – shows location • 'wear' – 'I wear a coat'
of and off	• 'off' – usually shows disconnection; opposite of on, e.g. 'I ran off', 'turn off' • 'of' – a preposition, usually shows connection, e.g. 'the brother of', 'a part of'
whose and who's	• 'whose' – shows belonging, e.g. 'Whose pyjamas are these?' • 'who's' – who is
passed and past	• 'passed' – verb form, a variation of 'to pass', e.g. 'I passed him on the street' • 'past' – never a verb, but flexible; often used to describe history, e.g. 'In the past …' or as a preposition, e.g. 'I drove past the gate' ('drove' is the verb, 'past' describes the distance)

1 Use the words above. Fill in the missing words in the sentences.

(a) He must have *passed* her many times, but he didn't know *where* it was.

(b) She didn't know .... car it was that had sped ....

(c) The light was switched ....

(d) Where had he put the jacket he wanted to .... that night?

(e) There .... kittens in the basket, and a puppy ....

(f) '............... late,' she said, 'and you've lost .... scarf.'

(g) I knew .... him but we had never met.

(h) It was .... hot; if they went jogging they might have .... out.

(i) They had been over there, but now they .... behind him.

(j) .... other shoe is dirty ....

(k) .... idea is this?

(l) .... hiding in there and .... is my purse?

(m) .... never sure .... off on holiday and .... stuck at school ....

> Remember, an apostrophe shows a missing letter. For example, 'who's' is short for 'who is'.
> Try saying the missing part to yourself if you are having trouble remembering which to use.

SECTION B WRITING

Had a go ☐   Nearly there ☐   Nailed it! ☐

Common spelling errors 3

Twenty-one of the most frequently misspelled words are jumbled with incorrect versions below.

beginning   arguement   diffacult   disappoint
difficult   disappear   dissappoint
business   disapear   greatful
embarrassing   desicion   possession
weird   believe   decision
wierd   rhythm   independance
posession   embarassing   buisness
grateful   rythm   conscience   independence
experiance   beleive   conshence
argument   begining   occasionally   separately
reccomend   ocasionally   seperately
definately   experience   recommend   definitely
   conscious   consious

Guided 1 Match up the word pairs on this page. In each pair, there is one correct spelling and one incorrect spelling. Circle the correct spelling and cross out the incorrect spelling.

> Correct spelling can be learned. Every time you spell a word incorrectly, make a note of the word and start to practise the correct spelling on a regular basis. Try strategies like looking for a hidden word within the word you are learning to spell, or saying what you see.

2 For some of the spellings you are unsure of, make up a sentence with a tip for remembering the word. An example has been done for you:

I can recommend two 'm's in recommend ....

....

....

....

....

....

....

Had a go ☐   Nearly there ☐   Nailed it! ☐

SECTION B WRITING

Proofreading

Look at the extract from one student's writing below. Read it carefully, looking for any:
- spelling errors
- punctuation errors
- grammatical errors – e.g. misused, repeated or missing words.

> Remember that proofreading is important: 10% of your marks in Paper 1 and 10% of your marks in Paper 2 are awarded for AO6 so plan your time carefully so you have time to check your work for errors.

For AO6, you must use a range of vocabulary and sentence structures for clarity, purpose and effect, with accurate spelling and punctuation.

1. Circle and correct all the errors you can find. One example has been circled for you.

> Travelling through the mountains was the most incredible thing Ive ever experienced – and the most terrifying? The views (where) superb but we drove on the edge of the cliff. The road just fell away beside us and the road was on stilts. It felt like any moment the stilts would splinter like matchsticks and weed plunge down the mountain side.
>
> Of course it didn't help that my little brother was in the car. Moaning, wining, and then – just for good measure – singing. All I wanted to do was stick in my headphones but I had to talk to him to stop Mum getting distracted wile driving.
>
> When it got dark, the valley was an ocean below us and we drove alongside it, watching out for pinpricks of lite going passed in the pitch black. The quite was deafening, but beautiful it was defiantly one of the most memorable nights of my life.

Guided 2. Look back at three or four pieces of writing you have completed recently. How many errors can you find? In the table below, note down words which you have misspelled and the kinds of punctuation and grammatical errors you have made.

Spelling errors	Punctuation errors	Grammatical errors

> Practise looking out for the kinds of punctuation and grammatical errors you know you make regularly. When you sense you might have gone wrong, stop! Don't get lazy when you are tired near the end of an exam – double and triple check and correct any mistakes.

Guided 3. Use the space below to practise and learn all the spellings you have noted in the table.

SECTION B WRITING

Had a go ☐ Nearly there ☐ Nailed it! ☐

Putting it into practice

Answer the exam-style question below. Focus in particular on varying your sentences for effect. When you have written your answer, give it a thorough proofread. Use a different colour pen to correct any spelling, punctuation and grammatical errors you have made.

Paper 2

5 'Children who choose to work should expect to be paid less than an adult for the same job.'

Write an article for a national newspaper in which you explain your point of view on this statement.

(40 marks)

> When you tackle any writing question in the exam, you should think about sentence variety. Remember to:
> - use a range of sentence types
> - start your sentences in a range of different ways
> - structure your sentences for effect
> - avoid overloading individual sentences with too much information.

> **Remember:** You have more space than this to answer your question in the exam. Use your own paper to finish your answer to the question above.

Cut along the dotted lines and staple the texts together to make your own handy anthology. Make sure you keep it safe with your Workbook.

SOURCES

Source 1

The novel Rebecca *was written by Daphne du Maurier in 1938. Its unnamed narrator tells the story of her marriage being overshadowed by the memory of her husband's ex-wife, who died in unexpected circumstances.*

Rebecca

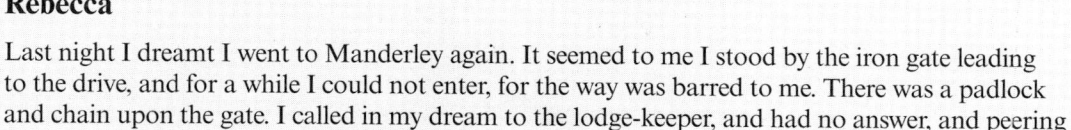

Last night I dreamt I went to Manderley again. It seemed to me I stood by the iron gate leading to the drive, and for a while I could not enter, for the way was barred to me. There was a padlock and chain upon the gate. I called in my dream to the lodge-keeper, and had no answer, and peering closer through the rusted spokes of the gate I saw that the lodge was uninhabited.

No smoke came from the chimney, and the little lattice[1] windows gaped forlorn. Then, like all dreamers, I was possessed of a sudden with supernatural powers and passed like a spirit through the barrier before me. The drive wound away in front of me, twisting and turning as it had always done, but as I advanced I was aware that a change had come upon it; it was narrow and unkempt, not the drive that we had known. At first I was puzzled and did not understand, and it was only when I bent my head to avoid the low swinging branch of a tree that I realised what had happened. Nature had come into her own again and, little by little, in her stealthy, insidious[2] way had encroached upon the drive with long, tenacious[3] fingers. The woods, always a menace even in the past, had triumphed in the end. They crowded, dark and uncontrolled, to the borders of the drive. The beeches with white, naked limbs leant close to one another, their branches intermingled in a strange embrace, making a vault above my head like the archway of a church. And there were other trees as well, trees that I did not recognise, squat oaks and tortured elms that straggled cheek by jowl[4] with the beeches, and had thrust themselves out of the quiet earth, along with monster shrubs and plants, none of which I remembered.

The drive was a ribbon now, a thread of its former self, with gravel surface gone, and choked with grass and moss. The trees had thrown out low branches, making an impediment to progress; the gnarled roots looked like skeleton claws. Scattered here and again amongst this jungle growth I would recognise shrubs that had been landmarks in our time, things of culture and grace, hydrangeas whose blue heads had been famous. No hand had checked their progress, and they had gone native now, rearing to monster height without a bloom, black and ugly as the nameless parasites that grew beside them.

On and on, now east now west, wound the poor thread that once had been our drive. Sometimes I thought it lost, but it appeared again, beneath a fallen tree perhaps, or struggling on the other side of a muddied ditch created by the winter rains. I had not thought the way so long. Surely the miles had multiplied, even as the trees had done, and this path led but to a labyrinth[5], some choked wilderness, and not to the house at all. I came upon it suddenly; the approach masked by the unnatural growth of a vast shrub that spread in all directions, and I stood, my heart thumping in my breast, the strange prick of tears behind my eyes.

There was Manderley, our Manderley, secretive and silent as it had always been, the grey stone shining in the moonlight of my dream, the mullioned windows[6] reflecting the green lawns and the terrace. Time could not wreck the perfect symmetry of those walls, nor the site itself, a jewel in the hollow of a hand. The terrace sloped to the lawns, and the lawns stretched to the sea, and turning I could see the sheet of silver placid under the moon, like a lake undisturbed by wind or storm. No waves would come to ruffle this dream water, and no bulk of cloud, wind-driven from the west, obscure the clarity of this pale sky. I turned again to the house, and though it stood inviolate[7], untouched, as though we ourselves had left but yesterday, I saw that the garden had obeyed the jungle law, even as the woods had done.

1: lattice: a pattern of diamond shapes
2: insidious: slow and harmful
3: tenacious: keeping a tight hold
4: cheek by jowl: close together
5: labyrinth: maze
6: mullioned windows: windows with vertical bars between the panes of glass
7: inviolate: injury-free

Source 2

The novel The Kite Runner *was written by Khaled Hosseini in 2003. Its narrator, Amir, remembers his childhood friendship with Hassan, growing up in Afghanistan during a civil war.*

The Kite Runner

ONE

December 2001

I became what I am today at the age of twelve, on a frigid overcast day in the winter of 1975. I remember the precise moment, crouching behind a crumbling mud wall, peeking into the alley near the frozen creek. That was a long time ago, but it's wrong what they say about the past, I've learned, about how you can bury it. Because the past claws its way out. Looking back now, I realize I have been peeking into that deserted alley for the last twenty-six years.

One day last summer, my friend Rahim Khan called from Pakistan. He asked me to come see him. Standing in the kitchen with the receiver to my ear, I knew it wasn't just Rahim Khan on the line. It was my past of unatoned sins. After I hung up, I went for a walk along Spreckels Lake on the northern edge of Golden Gate Park. The early-afternoon sun sparkled on the water where dozens of miniature boats sailed, propelled by a crisp breeze. Then I glanced up and saw a pair of kites, red with long blue tails, soaring in the sky. They danced high above the trees on the west end of the park, over the windmills, floating side by side like a pair of eyes looking down on San Francisco, the city I now call home. And suddenly Hassan's voice whispered in my head: For you, a thousand times over. Hassan the harelipped kite runner.

I sat on a park bench near a willow tree. I thought about something Rahim Khan said just before he hung up, almost as an afterthought. There is a way to be good again. I looked up at those twin kites. I thought about Hassan. Thought about Baba. Ali. Kabul. I thought of the life I had lived until the winter of 1975 came along and changed everything. And made me what I am today.

TWO

When we were children, Hassan and I used to climb the poplar trees in the driveway of my father's house and annoy our neighbours by reflecting sunlight into their homes with a shard of mirror. We would sit across from each other on a pair of high branches, our naked feet dangling, our trouser pockets filled with dried mulberries and walnuts. We took turns with the mirror as we ate mulberries, pelted each other with them, giggling, laughing. I can still see Hassan up on that tree, sunlight flickering through the leaves on his almost perfectly round face, a face like a Chinese doll chiselled from hardwood: his flat, broad nose and slanting, narrow eyes like bamboo leaves, eyes that looked, depending on the light, gold, green, even sapphire. I can still see his tiny low-set ears and that pointed stub of a chin, a meaty appendage that looked like it was added as a mere afterthought. And the cleft lip, just left of midline, where the Chinese doll maker's instrument may have slipped, or perhaps he had simply grown tired and careless.

Sometimes, up in those trees, I talked Hassan into firing walnuts with his slingshot at the neighbour's one-eyed German shepherd. Hassan never wanted to, but if I asked, really asked, he wouldn't deny me. Hassan never denied me anything. And he was deadly with his slingshot. Hassan's father, Ali, used to catch us and get mad, or as mad as someone as gentle as Ali could ever get. He would wag his finger and wave us down from the tree. He would take the mirror and tell us what his mother had told him, that the devil shone mirrors too, shone them to distract Muslims during prayer. "And he laughs while he does it," he always added, scowling at his son.

'Yes, Father,' Hassan would mumble, looking down at his feet. But he never told on me. Never told that the mirror, like shooting walnuts at the neighbour's dog, was always my idea.

The poplar trees lined the redbrick driveway, which led to a pair of wrought-iron gates. They in turn opened into an extension of the driveway into my father's estate. The house sat on the left side of the brick path, the backyard at the end of it.

Cut along the dotted lines and staple the texts together to make your own handy anthology. Make sure you keep it safe with your Workbook.

SOURCES

Source 3

Charlotte Perkins Gilman's 'The Yellow Wallpaper' was written in 1892. The narrator is undergoing the 'rest cure', common at the end of the century, when people with depression were told that complete rest – no activity at all – would help them to recover.

The Yellow Wallpaper

John laughs at me, of course, but one expects that in marriage.

John is practical in the extreme. He has no patience with faith, an intense horror of superstition, and he scoffs openly at any talk of things not to be felt and seen and put down in figures.

John is a physician, and PERHAPS – (I would not say it to a living soul, of course, but this is dead paper and a great relief to my mind) – PERHAPS that is one reason I do not get well faster.

You see he does not believe I am sick!

And what can one do?

If a physician of high standing, and one's own husband, assures friends and relatives that there is really nothing the matter with one but temporary nervous depression – a slight hysterical tendency – what is one to do?

My brother is also a physician, and also of high standing, and he says the same thing.

So I take phosphates[1] or phosphites – whichever it is, and tonics, and journeys, and air, and exercise, and am absolutely forbidden to 'work' until I am well again.

Personally, I disagree with their ideas.

Personally, I believe that congenial[2] work, with excitement and change, would do me good.

But what is one to do?

I did write for a while in spite of them; but it DOES exhaust me a good deal – having to be so sly about it, or else meet with heavy opposition.

I sometimes fancy that in my condition if I had less opposition and more society and stimulus[3] – but John says the very worst thing I can do is to think about my condition, and I confess it always makes me feel bad.

So I will let it alone and talk about the house.

The most beautiful place! It is quite alone, standing well back from the road, quite three miles from the village. It makes me think of English places that you read about, for there are hedges and walls and gates that lock, and lots of separate little houses for the gardeners and people.

There is a DELICIOUS garden! I never saw such a garden – large and shady, full of box-bordered paths, and lined with long grape-covered arbours with seats under them.

There were greenhouses, too, but they are all broken now.

There was some legal trouble, I believe, something about the heirs and coheirs; anyhow, the place has been empty for years.

That spoils my ghostliness, I am afraid, but I don't care – there is something strange about the house – I can feel it.

I even said so to John one moonlight evening, but he said what I felt was a DRAUGHT, and shut the window.

I get unreasonably angry with John sometimes. I'm sure I never used to be so sensitive. I think it is due to this nervous condition.

But John says if I feel so, I shall neglect proper self-control; so I take pains to control myself – before him, at least, and that makes me very tired.

I don't like our room a bit. I wanted one downstairs that opened on the piazza[4] and had roses all over the window, and such pretty old-fashioned chintz[5] hangings! but John would not hear of it.

He said there was only one window and not room for two beds, and no near room for him if he took another.

He is very careful and loving, and hardly lets me stir without special direction.

1: phosphates: a chemical used in the late 1800s to treat depression
2: congenial: warm and friendly
3: stimulus: something that creates activity or energy
4: piazza: a square patio space
5: chintz: a printed, patterned fabric

SOURCES Cut along the dotted lines and staple the texts together to make your own handy anthology. Make sure you keep it safe with your Workbook.

Source 4

This short story was published in 1950 by Ray Bradbury, often considered a science-fiction writer.

There Will Come Soft Rains

In the living room the voice-clock sang, Tick-tock, seven o'clock, time to get up, time to get up, seven o'clock! as if it were afraid nobody would. The morning house lay empty. The clock ticked on, repeating and repeating its sounds into the emptiness. Seven-nine, breakfast time, seven-nine!

In the kitchen the breakfast stove gave a hissing sigh and ejected from its warm interior eight pieces of perfectly browned toast, eight eggs sunnyside up, sixteen slices of bacon, two coffees, and two cool glasses of milk.

'Today is August 4, 2026,' said a second voice from the kitchen ceiling., 'in the city of Allendale, California.' It repeated the date three times for memory's sake. 'Today is Mr. Featherstone's birthday. Today is the anniversary of Tilita's marriage. Insurance is payable, as are the water, gas, and light bills.'

Somewhere in the walls, relays clicked, memory tapes glided under electric eyes.

Eight-one, tick-tock, eight-one o'clock, off to school, off to work, run, run, eight-one! But no doors slammed, no carpets took the soft tread of rubber heels. It was raining outside. The weather box on the front door sang quietly: 'Rain, rain, go away; rubbers, raincoats for today …' And the rain tapped on the empty house, echoing.

Outside, the garage chimed and lifted its door to reveal the waiting car. After a long wait the door swung down again.

At eight-thirty the eggs were shrivelled and the toast was like stone. An aluminium wedge scraped them down a metal throat which digested and flushed them away to the distant sea. The dirty dishes were dropped into a hot washer and emerged twinkling dry.

Nine-fifteen, sang the clock, time to clean. Out of warrens in the wall, tiny robot mice darted. The rooms were acrawl with the small cleaning animals, all rubber and metal. They thudded against chairs, whirling their moustached runners, kneading the rug nap, sucking gently at hidden dust. Then, like mysterious invaders, they popped into their burrows. Their pink electric eyes faded. The house was clean.

Ten o'clock. The sun came out from behind the rain. The house stood alone in a city of rubble and ashes. This was the one house left standing. At night the ruined city gave off a radioactive glow which could be seen for miles.

Ten-fifteen. The garden sprinklers whirled up in golden founts, filling the soft morning air with scatterings of brightness. The water pelted windowpanes, running down the charred west side where the house had been burned evenly free of its white paint. The entire west face of the house was black, save for five places. Here the silhouette in paint of a man mowing a lawn. Here, as in a photograph, a woman bent to pick flowers. Still farther over, their images burned on wood in one titanic instant, a small boy, hands flung into the air; higher up, the image of thrown ball, and opposite him a girl, hand raised to catch a ball which never came down. The five spots of paint – the man, the woman, the children, the ball – remained. The rest was a thin charcoaled layer. The gentle sprinkler rain filled the garden with falling light.

Until this day, how well the house had kept its peace. How carefully it had inquired, 'Who goes there? What's the password?' and, getting no answer from the only foxes and whining cats, it had shut up its windows and drawn shades in an old-maidenly preoccupation with self-protection which bordered on a mechanical paranoia.

It quivered at each sound, the house did. If a sparrow brushed a window, the shade snapped up. The bird, startled, flew off! No, not even a bird must touch the house!

The house was an altar with ten thousand attendants, big, small, servicing, attending, in choirs. But the gods had gone away, and the ritual of the religion continued senselessly, uselessly.

Cut along the dotted lines and staple the texts together to make your own handy anthology. Make sure you keep it safe with your Workbook.

SOURCES

Source 5a

Arwa Mahdawi discusses the dangers of self-diagnosing medical complaints online. This article was published in The Guardian *newspaper in 2015.*

'Googled your cough? Is death now upon you?'

At 11 am I had a strange pain in my toe. By 11.05 I was convinced it was a brain tumour. By 11.15 I'd realised that, actually, my shoes were probably to blame, but by that time I'd already decided on the music that should be played at my funeral.

You may think I sound crazy but, actually, I just have a mild form of cyberchondria: a condition in which benign aches and pains are transformed into fatal diseases after a few minutes spent looking up symptoms on Google. It's a common ailment[1]: one in 20 Google searches are health-related and, according to a 2012 study, one in four British women have misdiagnosed themselves on the internet.

Google is well aware that it is now most people's primary healthcare provider and has started to better monetise[2], sorry, I mean 'manage', how we access medical information online. Recently, the search engine announced that, when you ask Google about common health conditions, you will be provided with the most relevant medical information immediately, through the knowledge graph, so you don't have to trawl through heaps of websites. This new data is currently only available in the US but will eventually be rolled out globally.

The knowledge graph is, more accurately, an answers rectangle; it's that box that sometimes comes up alongside your search results with time-saving information about whatever you were looking for. Basically, it's Google's ploy to keep you from leaving its clutches and clicking on links to other sites.

The fact that Google is injecting medical information into the knowledge graph is, generally speaking, a positive thing. It means you can be more certain the medical information you're accessing is accurate. An average of 11 doctors have vetted[3] Google's medical facts; each of the 400 medical conditions currently listed was then reviewed by non-profit healthcare organisation the Mayo Clinic.

But Google's medical intervention isn't without serious side-effects. First, it gives Google even more control over the information we consume every day. Second, by making it easier to research medical conditions, this new function is basically crack cocaine for healthy worriers.

Sometimes, Google's knowledge graph just doesn't have the answer and you will be tempted to click through to a diagnostic quiz. Online quizzes are a great way to find out which Disney princess you are (I'm Pocahontas) but they are not such a great way to find out if you are suffering from Asperger syndrome.

Indeed, it's possible that, by now, you are starting to remember that your toe hurts, or you have a headache, or your leg is twitching. You may feel an urge to Google your symptoms. Hypochondriacs, please proceed with caution.

1: ailment: sickness
2: monetise: make money from
3: vetted: inspected/examined

SOURCES

Cut along the dotted lines and staple the texts together to make your own handy anthology. Make sure you keep it safe with your Workbook.

Source 5b

> This is an extract taken from the book American Notes *by Charles Dickens (1842). At the age of 30 the English novelist Dickens made his first visit to America. Works such as* Oliver Twist *and* The Pickwick Papers *had already made him the most famous writer in the world. Here he describes his journey on the boat.*

The Boat to America

We all dined together that day; and a rather formidable[1] party we were: no fewer than eighty-six strong. The vessel being pretty deep in the water, with all her coals on board and so many passengers, and the weather being calm and quiet, there was but little motion; so that before the dinner was half over, even those passengers who were most distrustful of themselves plucked up amazingly; and those who in the morning had returned to the universal question, 'Are you a good sailor?' answered boldly 'Yes' and with some irritation too, as though they would add, 'I should like to know what you see in ME, sir, particularly, to justify suspicion!'

Notwithstanding[2] this high tone of courage and confidence, I could not but observe that very few remained long over their wine; and that everybody had an unusual love of the open air; and that the favourite and most wanted seats were invariably[3] those nearest to the door. The tea-table, too, was by no means as well attended as the dinner-table; and there was less card-playing than might have been expected.

Still, with the exception of one lady, who had retired at dinner-time, there were no invalids as yet; and walking, and smoking, and drinking of brandy-and-water (but always in the open air), went on with unabated spirit, until eleven o'clock or thereabouts, when 'turning in' – no sailor of seven hours' experience talks of going to bed – became the order of the night. The perpetual[4] tramp of boot-heels on the decks gave place to a heavy silence, and the whole human freight was stowed away below, excepting a very few stragglers, like myself, who were probably, like me, afraid to go there.

To one unaccustomed to such scenes, this is a very striking time on shipboard. Afterwards, and when its novelty had long worn off, it never ceased to have a peculiar interest and charm for me. The gloom through which the great black mass holds its direct and certain course; the rushing water, plainly heard, but dimly seen; the broad, white, glistening track, that follows in the vessel's wake; the men on the look-out forward, who would be scarcely visible against the dark sky, but for their blotting out some score of glistening stars; the helmsman at the wheel, with the illuminated card before him, shining, a speck of light amidst the darkness; the melancholy[5] sighing of the wind through block, and rope, and chain; the gleaming forth of light from every crevice[6], nook, and tiny piece of glass about the decks, as though the ship were filled with fire in hiding, ready to burst through any outlet, wild with its resistless power of death and ruin.

At first, too, and even when the hour, and all the objects it exalts[7], have come to be familiar, it is difficult, alone and thoughtful, to hold them to their proper shapes and forms. They change with the wandering fancy; assume the semblance[8] of things left far away; put on the well-remembered aspect of favourite places dearly loved; and even people them with shadows. Streets, houses, rooms; figures so like their usual occupants, that they have startled me by their reality, which far exceeded, as it seemed to me, all power of mine to conjure up[9] the absent; have, many and many a time, at such an hour, grown suddenly out of objects with whose real look, and use, and purpose, I was as well acquainted as with my own two hands.

My own two hands, and feet likewise, being very cold, however, on this particular occasion, I crept below at midnight. It was not exactly comfortable below. It was decidedly close; and it was impossible to be unconscious of the presence of that extraordinary compound of strange smells, which is to be found nowhere but on board ship, and which is such a subtle perfume that it seems to enter at every pore of the skin, and whisper of the hold.

Two passengers' wives (one of them my own) lay already in silent agonies on the sofa; and one lady's maid (my lady's) was a mere bundle on the floor, cursing her destiny. Everything sloped the wrong way: which in itself was an aggravation[10] scarcely to be borne. Now every plank and timber creaked, as if the ship were made of wicker-work; and now crackled, like an enormous fire of the driest possible twigs. There was nothing for it but bed; so I went to bed.

1: formidable: impressive/ intimidating
2: notwithstanding: despite
3: invariably: consistently
4: perpetual: constant
5: melancholy: sad
6: crevice: gap
7: exalts: praises
8: semblance: appearance
9: conjure up: make appear by magic
10: aggravation: annoyance

Source 6a

Jessica Valenti explores the way housework is not shared equally between men and women. This article was published in The Guardian newspaper in 2014.

Women aren't 'better' at housework – but men sure are better at avoiding it

Housework is boring, so it makes sense that arguing about it – or trying to battle the gender inequality around it – would also be pretty mind-numbing. After spending a day picking up socks, no one really wants to talk about who picked up the socks.

But caring about equality across the board shouldn't be a zero sum game, and women are not going to be able to make progress on more urgent and public and political issues if we're too damn tired from doing so much work at home.

So it will not surprise any woman to learn that the latest numbers from the US Bureau of Labor Statistics show that women are still doing a lot more housework than men – over three times as much, in fact. (We do twice as much in the UK, apparently, and a whole lot more than that east of Europe.) If your eyes are already starting to glaze over, you're not alone: every year, in every country, the same sort of statistics come out, and every year there are a few articles pointing out the disparity[1] and every year, in every country, nothing changes.

And while men are doing *some* housework – in Germany men spend an average of 90 minutes a day on domestic work, in Turkey just a measly 21 – it's not just mopping that needs doing. Statistics say that American women are spending about 6 hours a week on housework – but that's really 8.5 if you count household management. So it's not just physical labour – like vacuuming or scrubbing toilets – that's running us down, it's the day-to-day mental work. We're not just shopping, we're making the grocery lists. We're not just cleaning, we're figuring out what's dirty.

Thinking about doing chores may not *seem* like a lot of work – but consider what an incredible privilege it is to have your mind free of multitasking. Men who don't have to think about which chores have to be done and who is going to do them have the luxury of headspace to think more about work, hobbies or *any damn thing they want*. Women, meanwhile, are trying to figure out if the kids need any more juice boxes that week. (Speaking of kids, the latest numbers don't even take child care into account, a huge – albeit[2] cute – time suck for women.)

The more we all let men get away with saying that they just 'don't care' about filth or that women are somehow naturally better at picking up around the house, the longer the chore disparity will last. Yes, sometimes just washing someone else's dirty cup feels easier than making a stink about why it's been sitting on a dresser for two days. But rolling our eyes or quietly seething only ensures another, dirtier cup around the corner.

As boring as housework can be – as a literal chore or as a political issue – we can't continue to treat it as ancillary[3] to the larger fight for women's equality. What happens in our homes matters, as does women's time and how they spend it. It's core to feminism[4].

So women, let's remember that our unpaid labour is work too – and that we need to hold men accountable. Men ... just do the damn dishes.

1: disparity: unfair difference/inequality
2: albeit: even though
3: ancillary: additional
4: feminism: belief in equal rights for women

SOURCES

Cut along the dotted lines and staple the texts together to make your own handy anthology. Make sure you keep it safe with your Workbook.

Source 6b

This extract is from The American Frugal Housewife *by Lydia Maria Child, a practical guide to housework, written in 1833. This section gives guidance on saving money.*

The American Frugal Housewife

The true economy of housekeeping is simply the art of gathering up all the fragments, so that nothing be lost. I mean fragments of time, as well as materials.

'Time is money.' For this reason, cheap as stockings are, it is good economy to knit them. Cotton and woollen yarn[1] are both cheap; stockings that are knit wear twice as long as woven ones; and they can be done at odd minutes of time, which would not be otherwise employed. Where there are children, or aged people, it is sufficient to recommend knitting, that it is an employment.

Nothing should be thrown away so long as it is possible to make any use of it, however trifling[2] that use may be; and whatever be the size of a family, every member should be employed either in earning or saving money.

Buy merely enough to get along with at first. It is only by experience that you can tell what will be the wants of your family. If you spend all your money, you will find you have purchased many things you do not want, and have no means left to get many things which you do want.

Have all the good bits of vegetables and meat collected after dinner, and minced before they are set away; that they may be in readiness to make a little savoury mince meat for supper or breakfast. Take the skins off your potatoes before they grow cold.

Economy is generally despised as a low virtue[3], tending to make people ungenerous and selfish. This is true of avarice[4]; but it is not so of economy. The man who is economical is laying up for himself the permanent power of being useful and generous.

He who thoughtlessly gives away ten dollars, when he owes a hundred more than he can pay, deserves no praise, – he obeys a sudden impulse, more like instinct than reason: it would be real charity to check this feeling; because the good he does maybe doubtful, while the injury he does his family and creditors is certain.

It would be better to ensure that no opportunity for economy is overlooked. Use the shopping list for a family for a week to make sure nothing – food nor money – is wasted.

1: yarn: thread used for knitting, weaving, or sewing
2: trifling: unimportant
3: virtue: behaviour showing high moral standards
4: avarice: greed

Source 7a

> *Author Robert Hallmann offers a glimpse into how he creates ghost stories. This article was published on The History Press website.*

Creating ghost stories

Essex, in spite of its friendly and prosperous present, has an ancient history of Roman invaders and Saxon immigrants, Pagan[1] groves and Christian conversions, Viking raiders, Norman conquerors, Civil War battles and sieges, witches, witch-hunts and witch trials, smugglers on its convoluting coast and highwaymen in its extensive forests, not forgetting more recently Zeppelin disasters and bombing raids.

There has been so much personal terror, so much anguish, so much blood soaked into Essex soil, that it is perhaps not surprising that there are so many tales of hauntings, of supernatural sightings and unexplainable experiences. Can you imagine Valkyries[2] or witches riding in such a sky, on such a day?

Like a simmering undercurrent this past lingers on into the present. A writer just has to tap into that flow of evidence and it can read like stories. The lore and traditions are as colourful as any county's. At least that is how I perceive the tales that I hope to have added to its treasury. A tale may be new, but if it is set in a particular time and place, it – or something rather similar – may well have happened.

Way out in the estuary on a now quiet backwater I found a simple little sign on a post driven into a tussock[3] of blue mud at low tide with a message: 'Here a witch was swum…' That is all I remember, but what did it mean? What was the outcome? Few people survived such trials, as either they drowned, which proved them innocent, or they survived, which meant the Devil had saved them and they were guilty and doomed to be hung, even if air collecting in the many undergarments worn at the time had supplied the buoyancy. It doesn't make much sense to us, but such was the uncertainty in people's lives that such murder seemed logical. And in an otherwise empty landscape of a tidal marsh with only crustaceans and seagulls for witnesses, the mewling cry of some seabirds might well be mistaken for something more sinister in half-light or mist.

What dastardly crime could be waiting in such a setting? What could be lurking down that path? Could that be where the body was hidden?

You walk in an ancient forest and some of the weathered and pollarded[4] trees have grown into odd shapes. Often, with a little imagination, those trees can show faces, distorted like gargoyles or misshapen animals or humans. Would they frighten you if seen at the right angle and in the right light at a time when your conscience is troubling you?

Much depends on the mood we are in. At times of dread we are more receptive to stories and notions that may seem impossible, just as nightmares will visit more likely at such times. More prayers are said in wartimes and at the same time fortune-tellers, shamans and charlatans are sought out more frequently.

Sometimes we like to be scared by storytellers, or the modern day equivalent of television and films. Most of the Brothers Grimm tales are positively frightening. It is embedded deep within our psyche, that feeling of something outside of our control, lingering in a particular spot. Would you not expect someone or something to shadow you into that uncertain grey distance… some water sprite cling to your boots or leggings to drag you into that damp uncertainty?

I have been a life-long photographer – people and places, but especially landscapes have been my interests. Twisted trees and eerie scenes harbour their own attraction. Today, with the aid of Photoshop, we can add some extra frisson[5] to images that may add a touch of danger or mystery to set the imagination racing. Set in a time research has made familiar, mix scene and story into the cauldron, that's an interesting formula to me.

1: **Pagan**: relating to an ancient religious community
2: **Valkyries**: Norse female warriors
3: **tussock**: patch of thick grass
4: **pollarded**: where branches have been cut off
5: **frisson**: excitement or fear

SOURCES Cut along the dotted lines and staple the texts together to make your own handy anthology. Make sure you keep it safe with your Workbook.

Source 7b

In this extract from his book Extraordinary Popular Delusions *published in 1841, the Scottish writer Charles Mackay writes about the widespread belief in haunted houses.*

Haunted Houses

Who has not either seen or heard of some house, shut up and uninhabitable, fallen into decay, and looking dusty and dreary, from which, at midnight, strange sounds have been heard to issue: the rattling of chains, and the groaning of perturbed[1] spirits?

A house that people have thought it unsafe to pass after dark, and which has remained for years without a tenant, and which no tenant would occupy, even were he paid to do so. There are hundreds of such houses in England at the present day; hundreds in France, Germany, and almost every country of Europe, which are marked with the mark of fear – places for the timid to avoid, and the pious[2] to bless themselves at, and ask protection from, as they pass – the abodes of ghosts and evil spirits.

A house in Aix-la-Chapelle[3], a large desolate-looking building, remained uninhabited for five years, on account of the mysterious knockings that there were heard within it at all hours of the day and night. Nobody could account for the noises; and the fear became at last so excessive, that the persons who inhabited the houses on either side relinquished[4] their tenancy, and went to reside in other quarters of the town, where there was less chance of interruption from evil spirits. From being so long without an inhabitant the house at last grew so ruinous, so dingy[5], and so miserable in its outward appearance, and so like the place that ghosts might be supposed to haunt, that few persons cared to go past it after sunset. The knocking that was heard in one of the upper rooms was not very loud, but it was very regular.

The gossips of the neighbourhood asserted that they often heard groans from the cellars, and saw lights moved about from one window to another immediately after the midnight bell had tolled. Spectres in white habiliments[6] were reported to have gibed[7] and chattered from the windows; but all these stories could bear no investigation.

Accident at last discovered the cause, and restored tranquillity[8] to the neighbourhood. The proprietor, who suffered not only in his mind but in his pocket, had sold the building at a ruinously small price, to get rid of all future annoyance. The new proprietor was standing in a room on the first floor when he heard the door driven to at the bottom with a considerable noise, and then fly open immediately, about two inches and no more. He stood still a minute and watched, and the same thing occurred a second and a third time. He examined the door attentively, and all the mystery was unravelled. The latch of the door was broken so that it could not be fastened, and it swung chiefly upon the bottom hinge. Immediately opposite was a window, in which one pane of glass was broken; and when the wind was in a certain quarter, the draught of air was so strong that it blew the door to with some violence.

The new proprietor lost no time in sending for a glazier, and the mysterious noises ceased for ever. The house was replastered and repainted, and once more regained its lost good name. It was not before two or three years, however, that it was thoroughly established in popular favour; and many persons, even then, would always avoid passing it, if they could reach their destination by any other street.

1: perturbed: anxious or unsettled
2: pious: deeply religious
3: Aix-la-Chapelle: a town in France
4: relinquished: gave up
5: dingy: dark and gloomy
6: habiliments: clothing
7: gibed: mocked or taunted
8: tranquillity: peace and quiet

Practice exam paper

> The Practice Exam Paper has been written to help you practise what you have learned and may not be representative of a real exam paper.
>
> In the exam, you will be given space to write in. Here, you will need to use your own paper for your answers.

GCSE English Language

Paper 1: Explorations in creative reading and writing

Time: 1 hour 45 minutes

Instructions
- Answer **all** questions.
- Use black ink or black ball-point pen.
- You must **not** use a dictionary.

Information
- The marks for questions are shown in brackets.
- The maximum mark of this paper is 80.
- There are 40 marks for **Section A** and 40 marks for **Section B**.
- You are reminded of the need for good English and clear presentation in your answers.
- You will be assessed on the quality of your **reading** in Section A.
- You will be assessed on the quality of your **writing** in Section B.

Advice
- You are advised to spend about 15 minutes reading through the source and all five questions you have to answer.
- You should make sure you leave sufficient time to check your answers.

PRACTICE PAPERS

This extract is from the opening of The God of Small Things, *a novel by Arundhati Roy. Written in 1997, it is set in India and moves back and forth in time from 1969 and 1993. This section describes May in the location where the book is set and introduces the twins, Estha and Rahel, and some of their family members.*

Source A

May in Ayemenem is a hot, brooding month. The days are long and humid. The river shrinks and black crows gorge on bright mangoes in still, dustgreen trees. Red bananas ripen. Jackfruits burst. Dissolute bluebottles hum vacuously in the fruity air. Then they stun themselves against clear windowpanes and die, fatly baffled in the sun.

The nights are clear, but suffused with sloth and sullen expectation. 5

But by early June the southwest monsoon breaks and there are three months of wind and water with short spells of sharp, glittering sunshine that thrilled children snatch to play with. The countryside turns an immodest green. Boundaries blur as tapioca[1] fences take root and bloom. Brick walls turn mossgreen. Pepper vines snake up electric poles. Wild creepers burst through laterite[2] banks and spill across the flooded roads. Boats ply in the bazaars[3]. And small fish appear in the 10 puddles that fill the potholes on the highways.

It was raining when Rahel came back to Ayemenem. Slanting silver ropes slammed into loose earth, ploughing it up like gunfire. The old house on the hill wore its steep, gabled roof pulled over its ears like a low hat. The walls, streaked with moss, had grown soft, and bulged a little with dampness that seeped up from the ground. The wild, overgrown garden was full of the whisper and scurry of small 15 lives. In the undergrowth a rat snake rubbed itself against a glistening stone. Hopeful yellow bullfrogs cruised the scummy pond for mates. A drenched mongoose flashed across the leaf-strewn driveway.

The house itself looked empty. The doors and windows were locked. The front verandah bare. Unfurnished. But the skyblue Plymouth with chrome tailfins was still parked outside, and inside, Baby Kochamma was still alive. 20

She was Rahel's baby grandaunt, her grandfather's younger sister. Her name was really Navomi, Navomi Ipe, but everybody called her Baby. She became Baby Kochamma when she was old enough to be an aunt. Rahel hadn't come to see her, though. Neither niece nor baby grandaunt laboured under any illusions on that account. Rahel had come to see her brother, Estha. They were two-egg twins. 'Dizygotic' doctors called them. Born from separate but simultaneously fertilised eggs. 25 Estha – Esthappen – was the older by eighteen minutes. They never did look much like each other, Estha and Rahel, and even when they were thin-armed children, flat-chested, wormridden and Elvis Presley-puffed, there was none of the usual "Who is who?" and "Which is which?" from oversmiling relatives or the bishops who frequently visited the Ayemenem House for donations. The confusion lay in a deeper, more secret place. In those early amorphous years when memory had only just 30 begun, when life was full of Beginnings and no Ends, and Everything was Forever, Esthappen and Rahel thought of themselves together as Me, and separately, individually, as We or Us. As though they were a rare breed of Siamese twins, physically separate, but with joint identities.

Now, these years later, Rahel has a memory of waking up one night giggling at Estha's funny dream. She has other memories too that she has no right to have. She remembers, for instance 35 (though she hadn't been there), what the Orangedrink Lemondrink Man did to Estha in Abhilash Talkies[4]. She remembers the taste of the tomato sandwiches – Estha's sandwiches, that Estha ate – on the Madras Mail to Madras.

1: tapioca: a root of the cassava plant
2: laterite: a rusty-red coloured type of soil rich in iron and aluminium, formed in hot and wet tropical areas
3: bazaar: market place
4: Abhilash Talkies: the name of the local cinema

SECTION A – Reading

Answer **all** the questions in this section.
You are advised to spend about 45 minutes on this section.

1. Read again the first part of the source, **lines 1 to 5**.

   List **four** things from this part of the text that we learn about the month of May in Ayemenem.

   (4 marks)

2. Look in detail at this extract from **lines 12 to 17** of the source.

   How does the writer use language here to describe the old house?

   You could include the writer's choice of:
   - words and phrases
   - language features and techniques
   - sentence forms.

   (8 marks)

3. You now need to think about the **whole** of the source.

   How has the writer structured the text to interest you as a reader?

   You could write about:
   - what the writer focuses your attention on at the beginning
   - how and why the writer changes this focus as the source develops
   - any other structural features that interest you.

   (8 marks)

4. Focus this part of your answer on the second part of the source, **from line 21 to the end**.

   A student, having read this section of the text said: 'Even in this short passage, the writer is able to bring Estha and Rahel to life. You feel as if you know them already.'

   To what extent do you agree?

   In your response, you could:
   - write about your own impressions of the characters
   - evaluate how the writer has created these impressions
   - support your opinions with quotations from the text.

   (20 marks)

SECTION B – Writing

You are advised to spend about 45 minutes on this section.

Write in full sentences.

You are reminded of the need to plan your answer.

You should leave enough time to check your work at the end.

5 Your school or college is asking students to contribute some creative writing for its website.

EITHER:

Write a description suggested by this picture:

OR:

Write the opening part of a story set in a place that is very different from the country where you live.

(24 marks are awarded for content and organisation

16 marks are awarded for technical accuracy)

(40 marks)

Practice exam paper

> The Practice Exam Paper has been written to help you practise what you have learned and may not be representative of a real exam paper.
>
> In the exam, you will be given space to write in. Here, you will need to use your own paper for your answers.

GCSE English Language

Paper 2: Writers' viewpoints and perspectives

Time: 1 hour 45 minutes

Materials

For this paper you must have:
- **Sources A and B**

Instructions
- Answer **all** questions.
- Use black ink or black ball-point pen.
- You must **not** use a dictionary.

Information
- The marks for questions are shown in brackets.
- The maximum mark of this paper is 80.
- There are 40 marks for **Section A** and 40 marks for **Section B**.
- You are reminded of the need for good English and clear presentation in your answers.
- You will be assessed on the quality of your **reading** in **Section A**.
- You will be assessed on the quality of your **writing** in **Section B**.

Advice
- You are advised to spend about 15 minutes reading through the source and all five questions you have to answer.
- You should make sure you leave sufficient time to check your answers.

> *Before answering the questions, read through sources A and B on pages 118 and 119.*

SECTION A – Reading

You are advised to spend about 45 minutes on this section

Answer **all** questions in this section

1. Read **Source A**, *Easy Way to Stop Smoking* by Allen Carr **lines 1 to 10**.

   Choose **four** statements below which are TRUE.
   - Shade the boxes of the ones that you think are true.
   - Choose a maximum of four statements.

   A Carr believes it is impossible to quit smoking. ☐

   B Carr thinks the addiction is more psychological than physical. ☐

   C Carr thinks that you have to really want to stop to succeed. ☐

   D The writer gives three easy steps to stop smoking. ☐

   E Carr sees cigarettes as an enemy. ☐

   F The writer thinks that drinking alcohol is worse than smoking. ☐

   G Carr thinks it's okay to have the odd cigarette after you've quit. ☐

   H Carr believes that moping around makes you less likely to quit for good. ☐

   (4 marks)

2. You need to refer to **source A** and **source B** for this question:
   Use details from **both** sources. Write a summary of the different effects of smoking.

   (8 marks)

3. You now need to refer **only** to **source B**, the extract from *Manners for Men*.
   How does Humphrey use language to describe smokers?

   (12 marks)

4. For this question, you need to refer to the **whole of source A** together with **source B, lines 21 to 41**, Humphrey's description of manners and hygiene.

   Compare how the two writers convey their different feelings about smoking.

   (16 marks)

SECTION B – Writing

You are advised to spend about 45 minutes on this section.

You are reminded of the need to plan your answer.

You should write in full sentences.

You should leave enough time to check your work at the end.

5 'Smoking should be banned completely. How can the government allow people to do something that will eventually kill them?'

Write an article for your school magazine in which you explain your point of view on this statement.

(24 marks are awarded for content and organisation

16 marks are awarded for technical accuracy)

(40 marks)

Source A

This extract is taken from the self-help book Easy Way to Stop Smoking *by Allen Carr, published in 1985.*

Easy Way to Stop Smoking

It is ridiculously easy to stop smoking. All you have to do is two things:

- **Make the decision that you are never going to smoke again.**
- **Don't mope about it. Rejoice.**

You are probably asking, 'Why the need for the rest of the book? Why couldn't you have said that in the first place?' The answer is that you would at some time have moped about it, and consequently, sooner or later, you would have changed your decision. You have probably already done it many times before. As I have already said, the whole business of smoking is a subtle, sinister trap. The main problem of stopping isn't the chemical addiction but the brainwashing, and it was necessary first to explode the myths and delusions. Understand your enemy. Know his tactics, and you will easily defeat him.

I've spent most of my life trying to stop smoking and I've suffered weeks of black depression. When I finally stopped I went from a hundred a day to zero without one bad moment. It was enjoyable even during the withdrawal period, and I have never had the slightest pang since. On the contrary, it is the most wonderful thing that has happened in my life.

I couldn't understand why it had been so easy and it took me a long time to find out the reason. It was this. I knew for certain that I was never going to smoke again. During previous attempts, no matter how determined I was, I was basically *trying* to stop smoking, hoping that if I could survive long enough without a cigarette, the urge would eventually go. Of course it didn't go because I was waiting for something to happen, and the more I moped about it, the more I wanted a cigarette, so the craving never went.

My final attempt was different. Like all smokers nowadays, I had been giving the problem serious thought. Up to then, whenever I failed, I had consoled myself with the thought that it would be easier next time. It had never occurred to me that I would have to go on smoking the rest of my life. This latter thought filled me with horror and started me thinking very deeply about the subject.

Instead of lighting up cigarettes subconsciously, I began to analyse my feelings as I was smoking them. This confirmed what I already knew, I wasn't enjoying them, and they were filthy and disgusting. I started looking at non-smokers. Until then I had always regarded non-smokers as wishy-washy, unsociable, finicky[1] people. However, when I examined them they appeared, if anything, stronger and more relaxed. They appeared to be able to cope with the stresses and strains of life, and they seemed to enjoy social functions more than the smokers. They certainly had more sparkle and zest than smokers. I started talking to ex-smokers. Up to this point I had regarded ex-smokers as people who had been forced to give up smoking for health and money reasons and who were always secretly longing for a cigarette. A few did say, 'You get the odd pangs, but they are so few and far between they aren't worth bothering about.' But most said, 'Miss it? You must be joking. I have never felt better in my life.'

1: finicky: fussy

This extract is about smoking and hygiene, taken from an instruction guide called Manners for Men *written by Mrs C.E. Humphrey in 1897.*

Source B

Manners for Men

The good manners in this, as in many other matters, has quite altered during the last few years. At one time it was considered a sign of infamously bad taste to smoke in the presence of women in any circumstances. But it is now no longer so. So many women smoke themselves, that in some houses even the drawing-room is thrown open to Princess Nicotine.

The example of the Prince of Wales has been largely instrumental in sweeping away the old restrictions. He smokes almost continually. On one occasion, at the Ranelagh Club, I noticed that he consumed four cigars in rapid succession, almost without five minutes' interval between them. The only time that he left off smoking, during the three hours that he remained in the Pavilion with the Princess and other ladies, was for ten minutes when tea was handed round.

It is now no uncommon thing to see a man in evening dress smoking in a brougham[1] with a lady on their way to opera, theatre, or dinner engagement. This is going rather far, for a woman's evening dress implies shut windows, except in the height of summer, and her garments become as much impregnated with the odour of tobacco as if she had herself been smoking.

Some men have a knack of ridding their clothes and themselves of the fumes of smoke in a wonderful way. Perhaps one reason for this is that the tobacco they use is of a mild sort. Perhaps the diligent use of the clothes brush is another. But there are also men round whom cling the odours of stale tobacco with a very disagreeable constancy.

Why it should be so I cannot pretend to say. It must be due to carelessness of some kind, and carelessness in such matters amounts to bad manners. Even to men who smoke – and much more to those who do not – the smell of stale tobacco is revolting. Fancy, then, how it must offend the olfactory nerves[2] of women. Such men suggest the stableyard while they are yet several yards away!

A very delicate, even exquisite, personal cleanliness is characteristic of the true gentleman, and more particularly the English gentleman, who is noted all the world over for his devotion to his 'tub' and his immaculate grooming and cleaning. This is not claiming too much for my countrymen. It is acknowledged by other nations that ours is superior in this respect. Once, indeed, I heard a curious comment. At a foreign hotel one waiter said to the other in their mutual language: 'What dirty fellows these English must be to want such a lot of washing! I've carried up four cans of water to Number 47 this morning!'

Sauntering up the street of a small German town one day, two English ladies saw, a couple of hundred yards away, a party of men standing admiring an ancient gateway. 'They must be English,' said one of the ladies; and before she could finish her sentence the other finished it for her in the very words she had been about to utter: 'They are so beautifully clean!'

1: brougham: a light, four-wheeled horse-drawn carriage built in the 19th century
2: olfactory nerves: the nerves that carry the sense of smell to the brain

Answers

SECTION A: READING

1. The exam papers explained
1. (a) Paper 1
   (b) Paper 1, Section B
   (c) Read the extracts and make relevant notes
   (d) Paper 1, Section B
   (e) 10
   (f) Paper 2
2. (a) Non-fiction (paper 2)
   (b) Fiction (paper 1)
   (c) Non-fiction (paper 2)
   (d) Fiction (paper 1)
   (e) Fiction (paper 1)
   (f) Non-fiction (paper 2)
   (g) Non-fiction (paper 2)
   (h) Fiction (paper 1)
   (i) Non-fiction (paper 2)
   (j) Fiction (paper 1)
   (k) Non-fiction (paper 2)
   (l) Non-fiction (paper 2)
   (m) Fiction (paper 1)

2. Planning your exam time
1. 1 = C; 2 = F, 3 = A, 4 = D; 5 = B; 6 = E
2. Paper 1

		Marks allocated	Time I should spend
	Reading time		15 minutes
Section A: Reading	Q1	4	4 minutes
	Q2	8	8 minutes
	Q3	8	8 minutes
	Q4	20	20 minutes
Section B: Writing	Planning time		5 minutes
	Q5	40	40 minutes
	Checking my answers		5 minutes
	Total time:		1 hour 45 minutes

Paper 2

		Marks allocated	Time I should spend
	Reading time		15 minutes
Section A: Reading	Q1	4	4 minutes
	Q2	8	8 minutes
	Q3	12	12 minutes
	Q4	16	16 minutes
Section B: Writing	Planning		5 minutes
	Q5	40	40 minutes
	Checking my answers		5 minutes
	Total time:		1 hour 45 minutes

3. Paper 1 Reading questions 1
1. AO1(a)
2. (a) Language; children's fear (b) 8 minutes
3. (a) AO2 (b) AO1(a)

4. Paper 1 Reading questions 2
1. B, C, D, F
2. The following should be circled: 'I should spend 20 minutes on the question'; 'I need to use evidence to support my analysis'; 'I should refer to a specific section of the source'; 'I need to evaluate the text critically'.

5. Paper 2 Reading questions 1
1. (a) Question 2
   (b) 4 minutes
   (c) 8 minutes
   (d) Question 1
   (e) You shade in the box
   (f) They haven't shaded enough boxes (correct answers: A, C, D, F)
   (g) Question 2

6. Paper 2 Reading questions 2
1. Answer annotated: one source; all the text; key words are 'writer', 'language', 'viewpoints', 'housekeeping'; 12 minutes
2. (a) Order of bullets in the table: support your ideas with quotations from both texts; compare their different attitudes; compare the methods they use to convey their attitudes
   (b) Answer annotated: two sources; all the texts; key words are 'compare', 'different attitudes', 'housework'

7. Skimming for the main idea
1. Answer provided on page 7 of Workbook
2. The opening sentences suggest that the main idea of the article is that researching injuries or illnesses makes you worry, although it also suggests **that the article is about how these worries aren't well grounded and are the result of paranoia.**
3. For example: The end of the article suggests that looking up your health symptoms online **is a bad idea and you should think carefully before doing it.**
4. For example: The ideas expressed at the end of the article differ from those at the beginning as the beginning of the article focuses on the writer's immediate health worries while the focus for the end of the article switches to the reader's wider concerns about their health.
5. For example: The main idea in the article is that trying to diagnose health symptoms online will only cause anxiety.

8. Annotating the sources
1. Answers could include:
   - Word/phrase: 'sea' as a 'sheet of silver'; Technique: metaphor
   - Word/phrase: 'like a lake'; Technique: simile
   - Word/phrase: 'undisturbed' / 'inviolate' / 'untouched' versus 'jungle'; Technique: contrast
2. For example:
   - 'sea' as a 'sheet of silver': It suggests an **unnerving atmosphere: the sea is like a mirror reflecting the eerie moonlight.**
   - 'like a lake': There is a sense of **unnatural calm. The simile 'like a lake' hints at something lurking underneath the surface.**
   - 'undisturbed' / 'inviolate' / 'untouched' versus 'jungle': The reader infers that **the tameness of the sea and the unchanging nature of the house has been used to make the garden seem even wilder.**

9. Putting it into practice
1. (a) and (b) Answers might include:
   - 'hissing sigh' – personification and sibilance, suggests a tiredness or maybe something threatening
   - Repetition of time 'eight-one, tick-tock' is eerie and suggests **time is passing even though there is no-one there**
   - We know how many people are in the house because **of the number of breakfast items there are per person**
   - List and modifiers (perfectly, sunnyside, cool) suggest **perfection and idyllic life**
   - Repetition of dates and events becomes unnatural, suggests slight control
   - The preposition 'somewhere' is eerie; it's hidden and unknown.
2. For example: Bradbury creates a curious but threatening atmosphere by gradually revealing that the house is empty. The personification of the stove with its 'hissing sigh' suggests a hopelessness, but also highlights the fact that there are no *people* in the house, just appliances. Although the preparation of breakfast, with the modification 'perfectly', 'warm interior' and 'cool milk', indicates that this is a perfect household, this is contrasted with the lack of people. The repetition of time 'eight-one tick-tock' is another unnerving sound, as time is passing without the people in the house. Bradbury uses anaphoric negatives 'no doors …

no carpets' to further emphasise the absence. He continues to use the sounds the house creates to draw attention to the lack of expected human sounds. It is the weather box, not children, singing the nursery rhyme 'Rain, rain, go away'. The verb 'echoing' creates an impression of emptiness.

10. Putting it into practice
1 (a) and (b) Answers should include three or four annotated words or phrases, for example:
   - 'so that nothing be lost' – suggests everything is useful and nothing should be thrown away
   - 'Time is money' – suggests the writer feels that spending time making things will save money
   - 'Buy merely enough to get along' – suggests the writer feels that you should be thrifty and careful with your money, not to rush in and spend all your money at once
   - 'no opportunity for economy is overlooked' – suggests the writer feels every chance should be taken to save money
   - 'the injury he does his family' – reinforces the idea that wasting money can hurt more than spending it.

2 For example: The writer has a strict attitude towards saving money. For example, she insists that 'nothing should be thrown away', which implies a disciplined approach to making use of all resources. Moreover, the writer believes that 'it is only by experience that you can tell what will be the wants of your family', suggesting she believes that saving money is something that people only get better at over time. These ideas are supported by the use of imperatives such as 'Take the skins off your potatoes before they grow cold', showing that the writer feels that the reader requires clear instructions about protecting their finances and that her way is the only sensible approach.

The writer also feels that charity begins at home. The opinion 'He who thoughtlessly gives away ten dollars, when he owes a hundred more than he can pay, deserves no praise' indicates that the writer feels it is foolish and selfish to donate money to other causes when you are already in debt. She feels that this may appear like a caring thing to do but cautions that it can actually cause harm to 'family and creditors'.

11. The writer's viewpoint
Topic 1: Sickness: Answer provided on page 11 of Workbook
Topic 2: Housework: For example:
- Source 6a – frustrated attitude displayed towards men who don't do their share of housework
- Source 6b – helpful attitude that suggests spending frugally becomes easier over time

Topic 3: Empty houses: For example:
- Source 7a – an encouraging tone showing the reader that a little bit of imagination can make the ordinary seem extraordinary
- Source 7b – sense of disappointment at the abandonment of the house (maybe slightly mocking of the tenants who won't even take money to live there)

12. Fact, opinion and expert evidence
1 **Fact**: something known to be true: Malala Yousafzai was born on 12 July 1997. **Expert evidence**: the opinion of a person or group with special knowledge about a subject: You should improve your diet and do more exercise to give you the best chance of living longer.
Opinion: something a person believes that may or may not be true: Ed Sheeran is superior to all other musicians.

2 For example: The writer feels that her habit of looking up her symptoms online isn't too serious.

3 'It's a common ailment': **Opinion**
The writer gives her opinion that looking up symptoms on the internet is a 'common ailment' to make it sound like a regularly occurring disease.
'I just have a mild form of cyberchondria': **Expert evidence**
Rest of answer provided on page 12
'… one in 20 Google searches are health-related': **Fact**

The writer includes the fact about the percentage of health-related searches there are on Google to help to show the huge scale of the problem of 'cyberchondria'.

13. Explicit information and ideas
1 (a) Answer provided on page 13 of the Workbook
  (b) The house **speaks the time**
  (c) The house is empty
  (d) The house is in Allendale, California

2 *Rebecca*
Manderley: is silent; is secretive; is made from grey stone; has mullioned windows; has green lawns; has a sloping terrace; is next to the sea.

'The Yellow Wallpaper'
The house: is beautiful; is alone, is standing back from the road; is three miles from the village; has hedges; has walls; has gates that lock; has separate houses for the gardener and the other people; has a large and shady garden; has box-bordered paths; has grape-covered arbours with seats under them.

The Kite Runner
Hassan: used to climb the poplar trees; annoyed the neighbours; used to sit on the high branches; used to fill his pockets with dried walnuts and mulberries; used to share the mirror; used to throw the mulberries.

'There Will Come Soft Rains'
The robot mice: are tiny; come out of the wall; clean the house; are made from rubber and metal; thud against chairs when they move; vacuum up hidden dust; pop back into their burrows when they are finished; have pink electric eyes.

14. Implicit information and ideas
1 **Extract A**
Answer provided on page 14
Mahdawi **looks up her symptoms on the internet and concludes that your imagination has the power to transform 'benign' symptoms into 'fatal diseases'. She implies that people who misdiagnose their symptoms are 'crazy'.**

Extract B
Dicken's shows genuine sympathy and concern for his wife and her **'silent agonies' and his wife's lady's maid who is 'cursing her destiny'.**
Dickens is experiencing very real, physical symptoms of seasickness; he is 'very cold', 'not exactly comfortable' and surrounded by 'strange smells', using his senses to emphasise the authentic nature of his discomfort.

2 Answers could include these key points – remember to explain them in a detailed paragraph:
- Mahdawi looks up her symptoms 'on the internet'/ Dickens sees the symptoms of the people around him ('a mere bundle on the floor').
- Mahdawi talks about imagination and illness, emphasising that it's all in your head, 'You might think I'm crazy'/ Dickens talks about the real physical symptoms of illness, 'an aggravation scarcely to be borne'.
- Mahdawi emphasises how common and public cyberchondria is 'one in 20 Google searches'/'one in four British women'/Dickens talks about the personal experience of seasickness, 'two passengers' wives (one of them my own)'.

For example: Mahdawi's modern method of using 'Google' to find out her condition emphasises that there is no physical proof that she is severely ill – it's in her imagination only. Dickens, however, witnesses very real, physical symptoms first hand. His wife's lady's maid is a 'mere bundle on the floor', which shows her condition is authentic.

15. Inference
1 Examples might include:
   A: Answer provided on page 15
   B: it's wrong what they say about the past, I've learned, about how you can bury it
   C: like a pair of eyes looking down on San Francisco, the city I now call home
   D: There is a way to be good again

ANSWERS

2 For example: The narrator writes 'the past claws its way out'; this is a violent metaphor which suggests the past is an animal or monster that is able to viciously come into the present.

3 For example: 'I talked Hassan into firing walnuts with his slingshot'/'he wouldn't deny me'.

4 (a) Hassan 'never denied' the narrator anything, which tells us that **they had a very close friendship, always playing together, but maybe also that the narrator took advantage of Hassan's good nature or naivety.**

   (b) Hassan was 'deadly with his slingshot', **suggesting that he practiced a lot and had an excellent aim.**

16. Point-Evidence-Explain

1–2 Evidence B is the most effective because it is an example of a pattern of three and therefore links directly to the point made.

3 Evidence: For example, she uses **the phrases 'your toe', 'you have a headache' and 'your leg'.**

4 For example: Explanation B is more effective because it is fully developed and more specific. This suggests that **the reader's condition is becoming more serious.**

5 For example: The word 'paranoid' implies that the reader is starting to lose their grip on reality. It gives the impression that Googling your health can lead to psychological worries.

17. Putting it into practice

1 For example:
   (a) Manderley has an iron gate
   (b) Manderley's gate is locked
   (c) Manderley has a lodge-keeper
   (d) Manderley's lodge is empty/uninhabited

2 Answers could include these key points – remember to explain them in a detailed paragraph:
   - The simile 'a jewel' shows the value of Manderley and its hidden nature; sea 'like a lake undisturbed' creates an eerie sense of calm; trees 'like the archway of a church' emphasises how it is like a shrine.
   - The two long sentences describing the garden as a 'jungle' show the never-ending impact of nature – it also implies that the wood and garden are exotic and strange.
   - The description of the 'untouched' house with its 'grey stone shining' in the moonlight and the 'mullioned windows' reflecting the garden is bleak and gothic, conjuring up images of ghosts.
   - The repetition of the verb 'choked' and the use of other verbs such as 'thrust', 'crowded', 'encroached', 'thrown' are all aggressive in their tone and create an impression of an unstoppable force at work.
   - Repeated motif of the moon – the 'moonlight of my dream' and 'silver' on the lake – evokes an impression of superstition; together with 'supernatural powers' which reminds us it's a dream, and creates an other-worldly or ghostly feel hinting at danger or even death.
   - The personification of nature, 'in her stealthy insidious way' and 'with long tenacious fingers' is unsettling and creates the impression that the narrator is not alone there.
   - The repetition of 'Manderley' towards the end of the extract shows it remains present and on her mind; 'our Manderley' hints that the even though it is abandoned, the people who were once there haunt her as much as the house itself.

18. Putting it into practice

Answers could include the following key points – remember to explain them in three detailed paragraphs:
   - use of rhetorical question to immediately involve the reader: 'Who has not either seen or heard of some house?'
   - repetition of 'hundreds' to emphasise the sheer number of empty properties
   - use of pattern of three and repetition of adverb 'so' in 'so ruinous, so dingy, and so miserable' to highlight the terrible state of the house
   - metaphor used to add irony to the foolish beliefs of the locals: 'all the mystery was unravelled'; the word 'mystery' is ironic because the answer is exceptionally ordinary – a broken latch meaning the door is swinging in the wind, and nothing to do with any supernatural occurrences
   - personification of the wind illustrates the sense of fear caused by the noises: 'the draught of air was so strong that it blew the door to with some violence'.

19. Word classes

1 For example: Noun – 'Brothers Grimm', 'tales', 'psyche', 'feeling', 'spot', 'water sprite', 'boots', 'leggings'
   Verb – As well as answer provided on page 19 of Workbook: 'embedded', 'shadow', 'drag'
   Adverb – Answer provided on page 19
   Adjective – 'frightening', 'lingering', 'uncertain', 'grey', 'damp'

2 For example: The adjectives build up a picture in a reader's mind of the transformation of the 'dirty' dishes **becoming 'twinkling' after going through the machine.**
   The machine strikes the reader as **very efficient – sending the waste to the 'distant' sea – but it is also threatening and human-like with its 'metal' throat.**

3 For example:
   (a) The action verb 'digested' suggests a human stomach rather than a machine, which reinforces the idea that the robotic device may become too powerful in the mind of the reader.
   (b) The verb 'chimed' is effective because it implies to the reader that the machine works like clockwork and sticks to a very rigid daily routine.

20. Connotations

1 (a)

boring	Answer provided on page 20
fight	**battle, violence, argument**
equality	**fairness, rights**

   (b) For example: 'Boring' has connotations of something dull and unimportant, and so the writer is able to argue that this isn't true – it is important and worth discussion. A fight is often violent and dramatic, showing how important women's equality is, and also contrasts with 'boring'. That equality is associated with fairness and rights suggests that what the writer is arguing is only fair.

2 (a) 'smouldering unclean'
   Literal meaning: Answer provided on page 20
   Connotations: … Describing the colour yellow as 'unclean' suggests **it is not a cheerful deliberate yellow, but is a murky smoky yellow that may instead have been stained by grease or nicotine.**

   (b) For example: 'repellent'
   Literal meaning: A substance that deters pests.
   Connotations: The wallpaper is so disgusting to her that is repels her like a pest. This also has connotations of the narrator being a pest herself.

21. Figurative language

1 For example: The writer uses the personification 'sang the clock', which has connotations of **a pleasant-sounding voice, a high-pitched but playful sound.** This suggests to the reader that the clock is **'behaving', or 'alive'; it is joyful, which contrasts with the absence of people in the rest of the house.**

2 It feels hard, rock-solid.
   It is unappealing – nobody would want to eat it now.
   It's been there a long time, maybe a few hours.
   The toast has been abandoned. The family isn't there to eat it but the house doesn't know that and made breakfast anyway.

3 The writer continues to make the house sound alive **by using the metaphor of the waste disposal as a 'metal throat' which 'digested' food. This continues to personify the house, and highlights the lack of people in it by making the inanimate objects in the house take on personalities instead.**

ANSWERS

22. Creation of character

1. The writer uses dialogue to imply that the husband cares for the narrator, as he uses the endearment 'dear' and discusses her 'strength', and ways she can get better. However, the narrator's tone shows that she is uncertain how much he cares, as she feels 'unreasonably angry' and 'basely ungrateful' towards him, suggesting that she doesn't think he has her best interests at heart.

2. For example:

Quotations for evidence	'unreasonably angry'/'never used to be so sensitive'/'I don't like our room one bit'/'he takes all care from me'
Technique being explored	Contrast
Explanation 1	Suggests that the narrator is confused but stubborn about how she feels
Explanation 2	Suggests the narrator isn't sure what has caused her change in mood

The writer shows that the narrator is uncomfortable in her surroundings. **The contrast between 'unreasonably angry' and 'never used to be so sensitive' suggests that the narrator is confused about how she feels, and isn't sure what has caused her change in mood. 'I don't like our room one bit' is a childish tone, making the narrator sound stubborn and as though she is arguing with her husband. The 'one bit' is particularly juvenile, creating an impression of her difficulty. Although 'he takes all care from me' could sound positive in that he is looking after her, the tone makes the narrator sound as though she does not value his actions.**

Or:

Quotations for evidence	'what is one to do?'
Technique being explored	Rhetorical question
Explanation 1	Makes her sound helpless and confused
Explanation 2	Shows disagreement with the advice that she has been given

The narrator's repeated rhetorical question 'what is one to do?' makes her sound helpless and confused. She also repeats the word 'personally', which emphasises her disagreement with her husband, despite the fact that he is a doctor, and also suggests that she is more interested in her own opinion. The narrator also comes across as secretive. She calls herself 'sly', and writes 'in spite of them', suggesting that she doesn't respect the advice she has been given.

23. Creating atmosphere

1. For example:
   'repellent' = **A substance to repel pests = She finds the room disgusting and hateful; she feels like a pest herself.**
   'smouldering' = **Close to burning = Suggests fire or smoke, which is dangerous and claustrophobic – suggesting she is being choked by it.**

2. (a) Action verbs: look, judge, confuse, irritate, provoke, commit, plunge, destroy, hate
   Adjectives: big, airy, barred, sprawling, flamboyant, dull, pronounced, lame, uncertain, outrageous, repellent, revolting, smouldering, unclean, faded, lurid, sickly
   (b) For example: Overall, the writer creates an atmosphere of foreboding and threat by emphasising the claustrophobic, imprisoning nature of the room.

3. The tense atmosphere begins with the curious adjective 'barred', connoting a prison-like room contrasting with the nursery the narrator describes. Further adjectives 'repellent' and 'revolting' heighten the sense of the narrator's disgust. The writer's verb 'smouldering' suggests fire, which is threatening and contributes to the claustrophobic atmosphere by suggesting smoke which chokes the narrator.

24. Narrative voice

1. • This extract is written in the first person: Extract B
   • This extract has an omniscient, third-person narrator: Extract A
   • The use of narrative voice in this extract reveals the narrator' own experiences: Extract B

2. The writer's use of first-person narration **enables the reader to experience their emotions as well as what they are seeing. When the narrator states 'It seemed to me', her uncertainty suggests that she might be unreliable and that we can't trust the memory she is recounting. When the narrator calls out – 'I called out in my dream' – it emphasises how alone she is there which causes us to feel sympathetic towards her. In addition, when the narrator says that she 'cannot enter, for the way was barred to me', the way appears barred to the reader too and we are willing the narrator to find a way through.**

25. Putting it into practice

Answers might include:
- simile – 'Chinese doll chiselled from hardwood' suggesting at first a look of perfection, and the way that his face has Chinese features
- simile – 'like bamboo leaves' creating an impression of the thin, pointed shape of the eyes
- metaphor – 'The Chinese doll maker's instrument may have slipped' telling us about the intensive damage to Hassan's face caused by his harelip
- physical description – 'naked feet' either suggesting being comfortable and carefree, or their poverty
- colour imagery – 'gold, green, even sapphire' indicating that the narrator thinks highly of Hassan, and admires his face despite his deformity
- verbs – 'giggling, laughing' tells us how much childish fun they had together.

26. Putting it into practice

Answers could include:
- adjectives/descriptive features – 'desolate-looking', 'uninhabited' – to create the impression of emptiness and loneliness
- anaphora/pattern of three structure – 'so ruinous, so dingy, and so miserable' – emphasising the destroyed exterior
- use of the senses including noise – 'gibed and chattered' – and touch – 'draught of air was so strong' – to create an impression of the supernatural haunting the building
- prefix 'replastered and repainted' to suggest newness or renovation
- noun phrases – logical approach of the owner, contrasting his rational response with the other inhabitants.

27. Rhetorical devices 1

1. For example: 'decay, and looking dusty and dreary' or 'strange sounds'

2. It encourages readers to look out for warning signs **throughout the text of unnerving happenings, whilst also making them question their own personal experiences. It sets the scene for the rest of the text and entices the reader into wanting to know more more about the spirits described.**

3. The writer lists some of the qualities associated with the stereotypical haunted house. The reader is encouraged to imagine a house that is 'uninhabitable, fallen into decay, and looking dusty and dreary'. This series of negative images, all included within a single extended sentence, potentially overwhelms the reader by giving the opening of the text a notably dark tone. The writer also **uses a supernatural element within this opening sentence, with references to 'midnight' and 'perturbed spirits', and the sibilance with 'strange sounds' gives the text an almost menacing, scary tone. The language is extremely descriptive and emotive, allowing the reader to mentally conjure images of the setting, placing themselves directly within the text.**

ANSWERS

28. Rhetorical devices 2
1. The writer's use of repetition implies that household chores are something that women **have to do continually. The writer repeats the pronoun 'we're' to express her frustration that all women have to spend much of their time doing, or planning, housework.**
2. For example: The phrase, 'Men who don't have to think' suggests that men have the freedom to spend their time thinking about other topics because women are doing all of the planning and organising on their behalf. This contrasts with the hectic schedule of women, who are not only doing most of the housework but are always thinking about what needs doing.
3. For example:
   - metaphor: 'time suck for women' – creates an image of a rushed and frantic lifestyle for women as it implies that childcare makes all their spare minutes disappear
   - colloquial language: 'kids' – used to make the children sound more like animals – a 'kid' is a baby goat, which exaggerates how difficult children are to look after.

29. Whole text structure: fiction
1. Answer provided on page 29 of Workbook
2. The fact that nobody eats the breakfast suggests **that the family is missing, and that it's unexpected because they didn't stop the house from preparing breakfast, wasting it instead.** The presence of robotic 'invaders' highlights the lack of **human and animal life by showing that the only things left in the house are mechanical and preprogrammed.**
3. The description of the family's burned shadows **is morbid and shocking. It reveals to the reader the brutal, immediate deaths of the family and confirms that there is nobody left.** The final sentence 'filled the garden with falling light' creates a mood of **eerie calm by contrasting the gentle description of light and rain with the harsh and brutal description of the dead children.**

30. Whole text structure: non-fiction
1. The headline and opening paragraph contrast the 'friendly and prosperous' present with a long list of violent events from the past. This is an effective way to start an article entitled 'Creating ghost stories' as it shows **that ghost story writers can draw on and embellish historical events for their writing.**
2. (a) Either 'vivid images', 'warnings', 'calls to action' or 'advice'
   (b) For example: The descriptive and emotive images at the beginning would be balanced well with similar vivid imagery at the end; a warning at the end would match the violent events described in the opening paragraph; ending on a call to action or a piece of advice would match the main theme of the article headline which is about the writer encouraging/advising the reader on how to create a ghost story.
3. The opening to the article introduces the topic of ghost stories in an engaging way through the juxtaposition of the 'friendly' present with the violence of the past. Hallmann further engages the reader by showing, from the first sentence, how the past can be embellished for dramatic effect. **By exaggerating history and building up the vivid imagery of 'smugglers' and 'highwaymen' throughout the opening paragraph, he is showing an example to his audience of his process and hints at the advice he will set out in the rest of the article. He uses the concluding sentence to sum up the whole structure of the article. The concluding sentence confirms this as the writer tells his reader to 'set' their story 'in a time research has made familiar' (as he shows in the first sentence). He then tells them to 'mix scene and story into the cauldron' which relates back to the middle of the article.**

31. Identifying sentence types
1. Sentence A is a single-clause sentence.
   Sentence B is a multi-clause sentence (subordinate).
   Sentence C is a multi-clause sentence (coordinate).
   Sentence D is a minor sentence.

2. (a) Single-clause: At 11am I had a strange pain in my toe.
   Multi-clause (subordinate): By 11.15 I'd realised that, actually, my shoes were probably to blame, but by that time I'd already decided on the music that should be played at my funeral.
   Multi-clause (coordinate): It's a common ailment: one in 20 Google searches are health-related and, according to a 2012 study, one in four British women have misdiagnosed themselves on the internet.
   (b) For example:
   - short, single-clause sentence hints that there is more to come and builds the tension in the article
   - long sentence suggests the writer has been busy and conveys time passing very quickly as much has happened in a short space of time
   - the multi-clause sentence suggests that the article is well researched, with a series of pieces of information linked together.

32. Commenting on sentences
1. The long sentence, and the use of repeated words in it, creates a building tension. The rhetorical question then has a strong impact on the reader – after the built-up tension from the long sentence, they feel that they might now be able to use their imagination to see 'witches in the sky'.
2. By presenting the subordinate clause in this way, the writer focuses attention on it. This has the effect of diverting attention **away from the fact that the stories 'may be new' (i.e. might not be authentic).**
3. By starting with several long sentences with subordinate clauses, the narrator sounds **as though she is contradicting the advice that she has been given in a more rational, logical way.** The final short sentence creates a contrasting impression of **petulance, or argument: she is suggesting she disagrees but will move on to something else.**
The use of capitals mid-way through a sentence **helps to emphasise the writer's viewpoint and justify her behaviour.**

33. Putting it into practice
Answers could include these key points:
- opening focusing on the location, and the unusual setting that makes the couple seem uncomfortable there, highlighted by the writer's use of rhetorical questions
- focus shifting to the husband, and the subtext of his controlling nature. The short sentences and rhetorical questions suggests the conflict between them and the narrator's helplessness
- narrator's repetition of her own opinion ('personally') and the repeated questioning, suggesting her helplessness and desire to be more in control
- shift to description of the room itself, focusing on the wallpaper and its disturbing, hypnotic effect
- the ending – hiding the writing that she has described throughout the source – suggesting that she has to hide everything from her husband, creating a sense of threat.

34. Putting it into practice
Answers could include these key points:
- descriptive adjectives and emotive language to show we cannot rely on our senses: 'twisted trees'; 'uncertain grey distance'; 'mewling cry' of a seabird in the eerie 'half-light or mist' can transform into something 'more sinister'
- contrast between real historical events (facts) and vivid descriptions of 'smugglers' and 'highwaymen' and 'witches riding' in the sky
- use of questions to show the reader how to use their imagination: 'What could be lurking down that path? Could that be where the body was hidden?'
- personification of the trees 'distorted' by 'a little imagination' into 'gargoyles or misshapen animals or humans'
- inclusive pronouns – 'to us', 'we', 'our' – to identify with the readers – the writer becomes very persuasive
- pattern of three used throughout makes the writer's viewpoint more memorable and persuasive
- hyperbole and repetition, 'so much personal terror, so much anguish, so much blood'.

ANSWERS

35. Evaluating a fiction text 1
1. (a) makes the narrator seem in charge; makes the narrator seem like he thinks highly of Hassan's appearance; makes it seem Hassan covers up/takes the blame for the narrator
   (b) Hassan seems in awe of the narrator; the narrator seems to use Hassan at times
   (c) the relationship between them is interesting because Hassan seems naive, but then the narrator also seems to like him a lot
   (d) the narrator might only like Hassan because he takes the blame for what they do

2. I completely agree with this view **because the narrator says Hassan 'never denied me anything', meaning he could always get Hassan to do what he wants. He also lets Hassan take the blame when his father finds out what they're doing.**
   I partly agree with this view **because although Hassan 'never denied [the narrator] anything' he still wants to take part and play with 'a shard of mirror' to annoy the neighbours and they are 'giggling, laughing' together.**
   I wholly disagree with this view **because even though Hassan 'never told on me' and kept secret the narrator's role in what they did, the narrator also speaks admiringly about Hassan's eyes 'gold, green, even sapphire' and his 'hardwood' face, which makes it sound like the narrator watches him.**

36. Evaluating a fiction text 2
1. Examples could include:
   - 'strange prick of tears behind my eyes' – overwhelmed by her memories
   - 'On and on, now east now west' – gives the impression of uncertainty, there is no clear path or route through (also, 'labyrinth')
   - 'not to the house at all' – uncertainty and loss
   - 'it appeared again' – despite the initial uncertainty, the path keeps reappearing, which shows the pull of Manderley
   - 'unnatural growth of a vast shrub that spread in all directions' – personification of the trees and plants which have a life of their own – branches are trying to block her view of Manderley, feeling of being unwelcome and haunted
   - 'heart thumping in my breast' – despite the haunting, she is anticipating what is next.

2. For example:
   The writer effectively encourages the reader to see the narrator as both uncertain **and haunted by her past. She says, 'On and on, now east now west', which hints at being plagued by uncertainty: she is not sure where the path is being led. This is reinforced with the imagery of a 'labyrinth': she is trapped in a maze and doesn't know where it leads. The narrator has a 'strange prick of tears behind my eyes', demonstrating she is overwhelmed by her memories. The trees and shrubs are given a life of their own – the trees have 'multiplied' and the 'unnatural growth' adds to the feeling of uncertainty, as if they are purposefully trying to block her. However, 'it appeared again' suggests that the narrator knows that the path will always be there, and despite the 'choked wilderness', it is inevitable she will find her way in her dream. The drive being 'the poor thread' is quite dismissive, showing the drive – and so also Manderley – has lost its grandeur and importance to the narrator, further emphasised by it 'struggling'.**

37. Using evidence to evaluate
1. Support: That he won't let her 'stir without special direction' shows he is **controlling everything about her, even her physical behaviour**.
   Challenge: The adjectives 'careful and loving' show her husband is **trying to look after and protect her, acting in her best interests**.
   Other examples could include:
   - The description of the room with its rings and barred windows suggesting either a prison or a playroom.
   - The description of the wallpaper as flamboyant (which might suggest old but originally impressive) and the contrasting lines that 'plunge off' and 'destroy themselves', which are more foreboding.

38. Putting it into practice
Answers could include the following key points:
- the peaceful calm atmosphere still present in line 30, but contrasted in the middle of the paragraph by the burned face of the house and the five silhouettes
- the shocking revelation of the shadows burned into the wall, particularly the emotive use of the children mid-play, killed in an instant
- comments on the previous foreshadowing, and that the death of the family is not unexpected even though the manner of their deaths may be unknown
- the remaining nature – the foxes, cats and sparrow – could be discussed either as proving the scale of the destruction (the entire city and all its inhabitants) or as suggesting that nature has survived, although mankind hasn't
- the use of religious language in the last paragraph might be discussed as suggesting the scale of the destruction and the metaphor of humans as gods, possibly suggesting that now other creatures will inherit the earth and become dominant.

39. Writing about two texts
1. For example:
   Similarity: The articles are similar in how they both speak about household chores and believe that all members of the family need to make a contribution.
   Difference: They are different in how the second article is a lot less formal and more argumentative than the first. It argues for the rights of women and them being allowed to use their skills in more important areas than just housework.
2. For example: Child's opinion on housework is much more old-fashioned than Valenti's. Child writes about knitting as a job and how the children and aged people of a family should get involved in this activity, whereas Valenti doesn't see it as a real job but rather as time-wasting. She would rather women make progress on more urgent matters of society than talk about 'who picked up the socks'. Her tone is angry and argumentative as she writes in a conversational manner where you can tell the writer is becoming more agitated.

40. Selecting evidence for synthesis
1. Use details from <u>both</u> sources. Write a <u>summary</u> of the <u>differences</u> between <u>the empty houses</u>.
2. (a) (i); (b) (ii)
3. Answers might include:
   Positive/negative effects of imagination: Source 7a uses positive imagery such as 'colourful', 'treasury', 'attraction'; also, 'dastardly crime' makes it sound exciting, not scary. Source 7b uses negative imagery: 'gossips', 'unsafe', 'suffered', 'annoyance'.
   The past: Source 7a – 'ancient history', 'the past lingers on', 'tales', repetition of 'stories', 'lore and traditions'. Source 7b talks about the past in terms of decay, 'ruinous', 'dingy', 'fallen into decay'.
   The atmosphere of a haunted place: Source 7a – focuses on 'hauntings' as being always in the background of your mind. Something 'lurking down the path', 'something lingering', something to 'shadow you'. Source 7b – much more gothic, 'rattling of chains', 'groaning' and 'Spectres in white habiliments'.

41. Answering a synthesis question
1. **on the other hand, by contrast,** unlike, **however,** yet
2. Using adverbials helps you link together the similarities and/or the **differences between the two texts**.
3. A, C, D. While quotations *might* be useful they are better used in the rest of the answer.
4. (a) Overview C
   (b) For example: Overview C shows an understanding of the specific difference between the two texts.

ANSWERS

42. Looking closely at language
1. (a) For example:
   Extract A
   Purpose: to explain to the reader why there have been so many 'hauntings' on 'Essex soil'.
   Language: 'blood soaked into Essex soil' suggests negative connotations of generations of bloodshed; 'personal terror' suggests that many people have a violent connection to the past; 'supernatural' and 'unexplainale' show an uncertainty; sensationalist, hyperbolic and entertaining tone.
   Technique: rhetorical question, repetition of 'so much', multi-clausal sentences, two sets of rule of three, sibilance (supernatural sightings).
   Extract B
   Purpose: set the scene, ask a question, question the reader about personal experience.
   Language: alliteration – 'decay', 'dusty', 'dreary' – which conjures a negative, monotonous, gloomy atmosphere. The pattern of three is also used here to create an eerie atmosphere. The language is extremely descriptive and gothic in tone. The writer alludes to 'perturbed spirits' and refers to the time as being 'midnight' – supernatural references/the witching hour.
   Technique: Rhetorical question, multi-clausal sentence
   (b) The language used in Extract A is more sensationalist, whereas in Extract B the writer is more descriptive which creates an eerier atmosphere. **The sentences in Extracts A and B are both long, multi-clausal and full of adjectives. However, Extract B has more negative connotations. Both texts use a rhetorical question to draw in the reader and use alliteration to make the descriptions of the haunted places more interesting.**
2. Extract A: more abrupt, more conversational, asks the reader directly, 'Can you...?' which challenges them to disagree.
   Extract B: one long, opening sentence, ending in a question that the reader can answer, relatable.

43. Planning to compare language
1. For example, for Extract A:
   - Tone: Answer provided on page 43
   - Rhetorical devices: formal language: 'an unusual love of the open air' – a delicate way of explaining that many people felt so sick they had to go outside.
   - Use of imagery: longer sentences with subordinate clauses deliver a lot of detail, which adds to the wise and experienced tone.

   Extract B:
   - Tone: Answer provided on page 43
   - Rhetorical devices: factual as it refers to a '2012 study', conversational language. Modern and relatable subject. 'You may think I sound crazy' – assuming opinion, aware that some people may think it is madness.
   - Use of imagery: images of illness are quite depressing, adds quite a serious tone to the article.
2. **… He describes in detail how it looks, feels and smells when he climbs below board. He likens the 'strange smells' to a 'subtle perfume' in how it is all-encompassing and clings to every 'pore of the skin'. Mahdawi shows her viewpoint in a completely different way; she instead uses conversational, informal language that is intertwined with the serious subject matter of illness and more factual points. She refers to recent studies in order to back up her viewpoint that she has a 'mild form of cyberchondria'.**

44. Comparing language
1. For example:
   (a) Imperatives: the writer sounds knowledgeable and **gives the impression of helpful advice**.
   (b) Direct address: by involving the reader directly it encourages them to think about why this issue keeps on cropping up.

2. For example:
   (a) Possible answers that could be ticked are A, B, E and F
   (b) and (c)

Create relationship with reader:	Instruct the reader:
Extract A: Direct address – 'you spend, 'you can tell', 'you will find'	Extract A: Imperatives – 'Buy…', 'you will find…'
Extract B: Direct address– 'your eyes', 'you're not alone' and 'let's'	Extract B: Imperatives – 'hold men accountable,' 'just do the damn dishes'
Persuade reader to agree:	**Explain to the reader**:
Extract A: Repetition of 'want'	Extract A: Repetition of 'want'
Extract B: Repetition of 'every'	Extract B: Repetition of 'every'

45. Comparing structure
1. Answers could include these key points:
   Opening paragraph: Structural techniques
   Extract A: Repetition of the time in the opening sentences; starts with short sentences; sentences gradually getting longer
   Extract B: Answers provided on page 45
   Opening paragraph: Effect
   Extract A: A lot of detail; comical but morbid at the same time; comes across as a hypochondriac; narrative voice starts to worry more; becoming less controlled
   Extract B: Gives the reader a sense of place; multi-clausal sentences implying a sense of a long journey; a calm, placid atmosphere
   Concluding paragraph: Structural techniques
   Extract A: Pattern of three as in the beginning; humorous tone of the beginning is maintained; exaggeration; long sentence followed by a short, direct sentence for emphasis
   Extract B: Vivid imagery; final line 'I went to bed'; complete contrast with the beginning
   Concluding paragraph: Effect
   Extract A: Humorous; call to action in the last sentence; warns the reader not to end up like her (imagining her 'funeral' in the opening); tone is comical as in the opening
   Extract B: 'I went to bed' creating finality; defeatist tone contrasting with the optimism in the opening; Dickens goes from being well to ill; the tone is one of tiredness and disappointment.
2. For example: Mahdawi uses many of the same techniques to engage the reader in the ending as she did in the opening. She uses a humorous warning to the reader to beware of the dangers of cyberchondria. The tone is light-hearted though still reiterates dangers of Googling symptoms. Her warning in the closing sentence is a call to action for her readers. In contrast, Dickens uses the ending to sharply contrast with the optimism of the opening. He ends by going to bed, a final act of defeat – 'there was nothing for it'. This contrasts with the call to action in Mahdawi's article. Dickens' vivid imagery to describe the movement of the boat contrasts with the calm of the opening. The tone is one of tiredness and disappointment.

46. Comparing ideas
1. **Main idea**:
   Extract A and B answers provided on page 46 of Workbook
   Language and effect:
   Extract A: The writer uses figurative language to **exaggerate the symptoms – the metaphor 'bundle on the floor' emphasises how unpleasant sickness is, suggesting the illness is so severe that sufferers can't even get up.**
   Extract B: Uses hyperbole, 'like crack cocaine' to further exaggerate symptoms.
   Similar
   Structure and effect:
   Extract A: Long, multi-clause sentences points to the lack of control the writer has over seasickness.
   Extract B: By introducing points in a list: 'First', 'Second', the writer shows control over the illness.
   Different

ANSWERS

2 Extract A: Idea/point: Answer provided on page 46.
Evidence: Answer provided on page 46. Explanation: This implies a frustration at events not going smoothly/a downward spiral of negative events.
Extract B: Idea/point: Answer provided on page 46. Evidence: 'This new function is basically crack cocaine for healthy worriers'. Explanation: The use of hyperbole to argue that checking symptoms online is as mentally addictive as cocaine.

3 Mahdawi expresses her feelings about how addictive and potentially dangerous Googling symptoms could be to a person's health by likening it to drugs, conveying her wary outlook on this idea. In contrast, Dickens uses his idea of seasickness to show how physically painful the symptoms can be; he can see how mentally draining seasickness is for the sufferers.

47. Comparing perspective

1 For example: Lydia Maria Child in *The American Frugal Housewife* believes that women should dedicate lots of time to housework. In contrast, Jessica Valenti believes that women are overworked and so men should do more to help.

2 (a) Answer provided on page 47 of Workbook
   (b) In 'Women aren't "better" at housework', Valenti, by contrast, uses informal language like 'housework is boring' to illustrate her strong dislike of it and make her viewpoint more relatable.

3 Answers should use one piece of evidence from each of the extracts and suitable adverbials. Answers could include these key points:
   - both texts maintain the same perspective throughout
   - Valenti ends with a colloquial imperative: 'Men … just do the damn dishes'
   - The American Frugal Housewife ends with the formal phrase 'It would be better to ensure that no opportunity for economy is overlooked'.

48. Answering a comparison question

1 For example: **Language and structure**
   - Use of rhetorical questions: **A** – 'What dastardly crime […]?'; **B** – 'Who has not either seen or heard […]?'; Similar effect – convinces and persuades the reader.
   - Use of repetition: **A** – 'could be', 'could be', 'could that be'; **B** – 'hundreds'; Different effect – A draws reader in and B uses to exaggerate.
   - Use of alliteration: **A** – sibilant sounds 'cru_s_taceans and _s_eagulls for witnes_s_es'; **B** – 'be_ll_ had to_ll_ed'; Similar effect – echoing atmosphere heightens the feeling of strangeness.

   Perspective
   A – negative language and imagery, 'empty', 'sinister';
   B – negative language and imagery, 'dusty', decay, 'strange'; Different effect, however – the word 'dastardly' in A gives a more optimistic tone.

   Effect on the reader
   A – Intrigue 'empty landscape', 'sinister', rhetorical questions, hyperbole; B Fear and intrigue by connotations, 'decay', 'strange sounds', 'cellars'; Similar effect – drawing the reader in.

2 For example:
   Both writers convey a feeling of emptiness. The connotations of the word 'tidal marsh' in Extract A create an image of somewhere uninhabitable. Similarly, in Extract B, the writer uses alliteration to achieve the same effect – 'fallen into decay, and looking dusty and dreary' – which gives the impression of abandonment. However, the writer of Extract B has created a much more disturbing tone, with further use of assonance – 'cellar', 'bell' and 'tolled' – creating an oppressive atmosphere and hinting at something supernatural lurking in the deserted houses.

49. Putting it into practice

Answers could include the following key points:
Source 6a, 'Women aren't "better" at housework':
- the writer has a frustrated attitude to housework and believes men are not doing their fair share
- colloquial language – 'do the damn dishes', 'pretty mind-numbing'
- facts – 'in Germany men spend an average of 90 minutes a day on domestic work', 'women are still doing a lot more housework than men'
- imperatives – 'remember that our unpaid labour is work too', 'just do the damn dishes'
- repetition of 'every year' and 'every country'
- short sentences used to summarise paragraphs – 'It's core to feminism'
- words/phrases with connotations of tiredness – 'running us down', 'boring', 'mind-numbing'.

Source 6b, *The American Frugal Housewife*:
- the writer feels that extra time spent on organising the household is worth it
- repetition – 'wants', 'want', 'want'
- formal language – 'he obeys a sudden impulse, more like instinct than reason'
- words/phrases with connotations of restraint and discipline – 'so that nothing be lost', 'Nothing should be thrown away'
- imperatives – 'Buy merely enough to get along with at first'
- direct address – 'If you spend all your money, you will find you have purchased many things you do not want'.

Comparison:
- both writers see problems in society with the way housework is routinely done
- the writer of 6b is more concerned with the financial problems of housework, whereas 6a's writer is more interested in gender equality and sharing the work equally
- both writers use imperatives to guide their readers
- 6a's tone is more colloquial, partly because of the time difference (present day) and partly because of the different expectations of formality in newspapers specifically
- the modern source uses more adverbs and adjectives, developing a colloquial tone and sense of guidance rather than instruction.

SECTION B: WRITING

50. Writing questions: an overview

1 (a) Answer provided on page 50
   (b) Answer provided on page 50
   (c) Paper 1 / Paper 2   (e) Paper 1
   (d) Paper 1 / Paper 2

2 (a) Answer provided on page 50
   (b) Answer provided on page 50
   (c) AO5 / AO6   (e) AO5
   (d) AO6   (f) AO5

3 For example: AO5(a): Write **clear, fluent and interesting texts that show you can vary your tone and style for different readers, genres, and purposes.**
   AO5(b): Arrange **ideas in a coherent, clear way and make sure the reader can follow your line of argument.**
   AO6: Use **interesting, ambitious vocabulary, and different sentence types, that are well-chosen for the text being written. Be accurate in all spelling and punctuation.**

51. Writing questions: Paper 1

1 (a) True   (c) False
   (b) False   (d) True

2 Story

3 (a) Narrate   (d) Describe
   (b) Describe / narrate (e) Describe / narrate
   (c) Describe / narrate

4 **Description**: Give details about the scene in a way that entertains my audience: Teenagers
   Story opening: Answer provided on page 51: Teenagers

52. Writing questions: Paper 2

1 argue, inform, persuade, explain

2 (a) local newspaper (readers)
   (b) article
   (c) explain your point of view

127

ANSWERS

3 For example: Positives
- The internet is a good place to meet new friends.
- Social media allows families and friends to keep in contact even if they live in different countries.
- Surfing the internet is no less productive than watching TV.

Negatives
- Some internet content is unsuitable for young people.
- The internet can distract you from getting outdoors and doing exercise.
- Sitting at a computer screen can be bad for your eyes and back.

53. Writing questions: time management

1

	Paper 1, Section B: Writing	Paper 2, Section B: Writing
Total time	45 minutes	45 minutes
Planning your answer	5 minutes	5 minutes
Writing your answer	35 minutes	35 minutes
Checking and proofreading your answer	5 minutes	5 minutes

2 Planning your answer (5 minutes, small segment); Writing your answer (35 minutes, large segment); checking and proofreading your answer (5 minutes, small segment).

3 (a) False (c) False (e) False
    (b) True   (d) True   (f) False

4 (a) Answer provided on page 53
    (b) Answer provided on page 53
    (c) Am I achieving my purpose?
    (d) Am I making a range of points or repeating myself?
    (e) Should I be moving on to my next point now?
    (f) How much time have I got left?

54. Writing for a purpose: creative 1

1 For example: See: **Fields stretching out; a tall castle towering on the hill; a pier; a row of houses**
Hear: … **Clattering of cutlery; birds screeching overhead; the thud of a ball on tarmac**
Smell: **Salt in the air; spring-time flowers**
Touch: **Springy grass underfoot; the scrunch of woodchips on a playground; rough stone**
Taste: … **Hot chocolate foam**

2 For example: He was angry: **Face reddened, every muscle was taut.**
She was nervous: … **She kept getting up to check the door, or the time on her phone.**
It was a hot day: **The ice-cream van had sold out.**
She was thirsty: … **She drained the glass.**
They were happy: **The children skipped down the canal.**

3 For example: Simile: The castle stood proud as a soldier and white as an iceberg.
Metaphor: A frosted wave of grass rolled across the horizon.
Personification: Staring down, the castle rose haughtily into the sky, wearing a necklace of icicles.

4 Walking quickly: skipping, running, pacing, **dashing, darting, hurtling, racing, hurrying**
Closed the door firmly: slammed, thudded, shut, hurled, banged
Shouted angrily: hollered, **yelled, screamed, bellowed, blasted, bawled**

5 Answers should:
- use the senses
- include examples of figurative language
- use strong verbs that show rather than tell.

For example: The castle was as **white as an iceberg and stared down at the town that had grown up around it over the years, crowding in. Anyone looking up at it would have shivered in the cold shadow it cast, feeling the same spring of grass beneath their feet that past invaders had trod, each soldier standing as proud as the castle did now.**

55. Writing for a purpose: creative 2

1 Examples could include:
- feelings: 'afraid' 'nervously' 'I don't want to' 'hands shook'
- figurative language: metaphor 'puddles of light', simile 'shook like jelly'
- the five senses: 'light on the ground' 'melted into darkness'
- language choice: foreboding hint about future events 'I didn't mean it', suggestion of a conflict to come either external with Jess or internal with self 'I don't want to…'

2 For example:
  (a) Shows **the fear in a more suitable way for the situation; showing rather than telling – there's no need to say she's afraid too.**
  (b) The common metaphor **makes this more cliché; try using something more individual to the character.**
  (c) The adverb **isn't necessary; the verb 'walked' could be changed into something which shows how they were walking, such as inched or tip-toed.**
  (d) The present tense **contrasts with the rest of the past-tense paragraph, so needs to be made consistent.**

3 For example:
  (a) The metaphor suggests **that there's not much light, making the reader wonder what might be hidden in the shadows.**
  (b) This creates a sense that **at some point soon, the narrator will be on their own, making us wonder what happens.**
  (c) Hints at what is to come **and that there is a conflict between the characters.**

56. Writing for a purpose: viewpoint 1

1 Examples of points **for**: Point 1: Young drivers more likely to drive under influence of drugs; Point 2: Young people more likely to have distractions such as loud music in the car.
Examples of points **against**: Point 1: Not all young people take risks – unfair to blame all for behaviour of some; Point 2: Many elderly drivers are still permitted to drive.

2 Answers will vary. Remember that you can make evidence up, as long as it is believable. For example:
Examples of points **for**: Point 1: 40% of drug users are under the age of 25; Point 2: More than half of accidents involving young people were because they became distracted.
Examples of points **against**: Point 1: A newspaper study in 2016 showed that middle-aged drivers actually take the bigger risks; Point 2: Statistics show that elderly drivers are often involved in traffic accidents.

3 Example **for**: Some people might feel **that young people will only become better drivers with practice.** However, **it is clear from the statistics about road accidents involving young drivers that they are more likely to be involved in a serious crash, more likely to speed and more likely to overtake on blind corners.**
Example **against**: Some people might feel **that young people pose an unacceptable danger to other road users.** However, **recent studies clearly show that only a small percentage of young drivers indulge in illegal behaviour such as taking drugs then driving.**

4 Rhetorical question and direct address: 'would you be willing for a young driver to drive your car?'
Repetition (of 'more likely'), lists, pattern of three: 'more likely to be involved in a serious crash, more likely to speed and more likely to overtake on blind corners'
Alliteration: 'patience for young people to practice'

57. Writing for a purpose: viewpoint 2

1 For example:
  (a) Answer provided on page 57
  (b) Risk of cyberbullying
  (c) Likelihood of being damaged, lost or stolen

2 Remember that you can make facts and statistics up, as long as they are believable. For example:

Fact	Point
Example given on Page 57	Example given on Page 57
Professor Brane and her colleagues found that 80% of lessons have been disrupted through mobile phone use.	Not only are students distracted by using mobiles, but teachers are being disrupted too.

ANSWERS

Fact	Point
There have been more than 15,000 reported cases of cyberbullying in schools in the UK.	Mobile phones in school could make it easier for bullies to pick on victims.

3 Answers should include annotations on language, register, adverbials, and facts and statistics.
For example:
Language: factual; subheadings and headings; careful use of figurative language; not describing; standard English
Register: Formal tone
Adverbials: Similarly; However; On the other hand; Likewise; For instance
Facts and statistics: 15,000 cyberbullying cases in the UK; Test scores rise by 6% in schools where mobiles aren't allowed; 80% of lessons are disrupted by mobiles; 25% students have lost or have had a mobile stolen.

58. Writing for an audience
1 For example: The audience is likely to be **adults of both genders, probably those aged over 25, although younger people may read the article if they have an interest in this topic.**
2 Answers should be formal and appropriate for a mostly adult audience. Non-standard English, including slang and texting language, should be avoided. For example: The films that children watch on the television might contain swear words, but I believe they are still high-quality entertainment.
3 Answers should be appropriate for a teenage audience, and may include some informal language although non-standard English, including slang and texting language, should be avoided. A variety of sentence structures and a wide vocabulary should also be used.
For example: ...
The worst type of homework I receive is vague, unspecific and lacking in focus; for example, 'Research the causes of World War One'. This homework, if you can bring yourself to call it that, is a total and utter waste of time.

59. Putting it into practice
1 Descriptive:
  - Audience: teenagers
  - Purpose: to entertain, to describe
  - Image: of the shipwrecked boat, a stormy sea, the shipwreck itself
Narrative:
  - Audience: teenagers
  - Purpose: to entertain, to tell a story
  - Voice: first or third person
2 Examples should be suited to the task chosen (describe or narrate). Techniques might include: metaphor, simile, tense, strong verbs, using the senses. For example:
Metaphor: The sea was an octopus, greedily grasping for the shipwreck with its watery tentacles.
Using the senses: The wave of silence was broken into ripples by the harsh squawk of a seagull.

60. Putting it into practice
Timing: Plan: 5 minutes; Write: 35 minutes; Check: 5 minutes
Topic: Banning groups of schoolchildren from shops
Form: Newspaper article
Audience: Answer provided on page 60
Purpose: To argue/persuade
Two points for my argument: 1. Less peer pressure to steal in smaller groups; 2. Will stop schoolchildren loitering in shops
One point against my argument: 1. May be cold/dangerous for those left outside
Any other key features: evidence, counter-arguments, adverbials, rhetorical devices

61. Form: articles
1 Headline B is the best as it includes a rhetorical question and alliteration to interest the reader and also indicates what the writer's argument will be without being insulting.
2 For example: 'Better things to do with your time' and 'Addictive as nicotine'
3 For example: Many of us spend hours every day surfing the internet **without even realising it. The truth is that we waste hours of our life looking at a screen, not realising that is bad for our health, destroying our relationships and preventing us from being productive.**
4 Professor John Smith from Bristol University says, **'People who went completely internet-free for a week found themselves more productive and generally happier than those who did not.'**

62. Form: letters and reports
1 Informal language: Ihateschool@emails.com; Stores shd b open on Sundays; Tons of; a load of rubbish; choice!
Incorrect use of word: However (also/furthermore); there (their); Yours sincerely (Yours faithfully)
Incorrect punctuation: 'rubbish;'
Irrelevant information: where I always get a bar of chocolate if I go in after school
2 For example:
Improvement 1: We shouldn't have to pay for what we hate
Improvement 2: Why school uniforms should be free

63. Form: speeches
1 (a) F, (b) D, (c) A, (d) G, (e) B, (f) C, (g) E, (h) H
2 Answers will vary but should include some of the techniques mentioned in Question 1. For example:
  - Personal example: My role model was a football star and he inspired me to always try my best, even though I was no good at sports.
  - Repetition: Sports stars give to charity, sports stars work hard and sports stars inspire people.

64. Putting it into practice
Answers should be suitable for an adult audience and should include:
- a title
- an introduction
- details of the current situation and some appropriate recommendations
- facts/statistics to support the recommendations
- a conclusion.

65. Ideas and planning: creative
1 Ideas will vary but should be focused on the descriptive option
2 Examples could include: Sound: police sirens in the city, lapping stream in the country. Touch: rough feel of cement, cold rain, hot air. Smell: petrol/fumes in a city, cut grass in the country. Taste: bitter taste of smoky air, taste of chocolate bar/food. Sight: example included on page 65.

66. Structure: creative
1 Answers will vary but should have circled a narrative viewpoint and should:
  - complete the narrative structure with a balanced amount of detail for each stage.
  - include ideas about creative writing techniques.
2 For example:
Exposition: ... **Paint is flaking off the front door. Walk into a cobweb that have to peel off arm. Can smell dinner cooking inside.**
Complication: **Opens door to find it's empty – kitchen looks left mid-cooking. Use metaphor or simile to describe the silence (like disturbing an abandoned dollhouse).**
Crisis: **Hearing a noise outside; going out of the back door into big garden. Use dramatic adjectives or verbs to describe movement and the thoughts of the narrator; focus on description and the way that the scene changes from inside to outside. See someone wielding a large knife.**
Resolution: **Twist – parent/sibling preparing food for party to welcome home. Choose a technique, and use it effectively.**
3 Answers should adapt the answer to Question 2 and follow the flashback structure given in the Workbook.

67. Beginnings and endings: creative

1. For example:
   One-sentence description of the storyline: Finding a key to a locked door that opens somewhere different every time
   Narrative voice: first person
   Where is the story set? A large grand house with lots of land; the other worlds fantastical
   Who is the main character? A teenage boy

2. Beginnings should follow the examples, and contain appropriate figurative language. For example: Conflict or danger: The key had been lost for decades, but now I held it cool and gleaming in my hand like it was brand new. Something compelled me to put it into the locked door, and nothing would ever be the same.

3–4. Answers will depend on the opening chosen for question 1. For example:
   Dialogue: A happy tone:
   (a) 'Guess it wasn't such a bad idea after all,' my sister smiled.
   (b) I hugged my sister and we both laughed, safe now the monster was trapped forever.
   (c) 'Good luck!' we called, though we knew that the ghost wouldn't need luck anymore.

68. Putting it into practice

1–2. Plans for the narrative should include:
   - some form of four-part narrative structure – either a flow diagram or a spider diagram
   - ideas for beginning or ending
   - details of narrative voice and creative writing techniques to be used.

69. Ideas and planning: viewpoint 1

1. Plans should include:
   - an introduction and a conclusion
   - three sequenced key points
   - supporting evidence
   - a counter-argument.

70. Ideas and planning: viewpoint 2

1. Plans should include:
   - an introduction and a conclusion
   - three or four sequenced key points
   - a range of supporting ideas and details.

71. Openings: viewpoint

1. For example:
   Rhetorical question: Is it time to call 'time' on alcohol?
   Bold or controversial statement: Alcohol is as dangerous as cocaine or heroin.
   Relevant quotation: Dr Smith states that 'Alcohol is perfectly safe when consumed sensibly.'
   Shocking or surprising fact or statistic: Around 38% of teenagers admit to reckless behaviour when under the influence of drink.
   Short, relevant, interesting anecdote: Answer provided on page 71 of Workbook

2. For example:
   Rhetorical question: Is it time to call 'time' on alcohol? Or is it time that people learnt moderation?
   Bold or controversial statement: People may claim that alcohol is as dangerous as cocaine or heroin, but they fail to take into account the higher proportion of people who drink safely compared to those who take drugs.
   Relevant quotation: Dr Smith states that 'Alcohol is perfectly safe when consumed sensibly'; however, people can clearly not be trusted to act sensibly.
   Shocking or surprising fact or statistic: Around 38% of teenagers admit to reckless behaviour when under the influence of drink, yet only 1% have acted in a dangerous or illegal way.

72. Conclusions: viewpoint

1. (a) Warning
   (b) Call to action
   (c) Vivid image
   (d) Thought-provoking question
   (e) Happy note

2. For example:
   Type of example: Thought-provoking question
   Good point 1: 'untold damage' underlines how serious drinking can be.
   Good point 2: ending on a question makes reader really consider the issue as they think of the answer.
   My version: How many more people need to be seriously ill, injured or worse before we realise that alcohol is too dangerous to be on our streets?

73. Putting it into practice

1. Plans should include:
   - an engaging title
   - subheadings
   - an idea for an engaging opening paragraph
   - ideas for about three sequenced paragraphs, with details of figurative language to be used
   - an idea for the conclusion.

74. Paragraphing

1. Point: 'Giving pupils the choice of where they sit may sound like a good idea but would cause confusion and disagreements'. Evidence: 'What would happen if ten students all decided they wanted to sit at a table designed for four people?' Explain: 'The teacher is the professional … they are there for very good reasons'.

2. (a) Explain   (d) Point   (g) Evidence
   (b) Evidence   (e) Point   (h) Explain
   (c) Evidence   (f) Point   (i) Explain

3. For example: As a diligent young girl, I often feel resentful towards teachers who make me sit at a table with loud, misbehaving boys. Recent OFSTED reports have made it clear that boys are far more likely to disrupt lessons, which has a detrimental effect on the learning of others, especially girls. While I understand the aims of the seating plan, in reality they are grossly unfair. To be clear, I am keen to get on with my work; why should I suffer by having to put up with the poor focus of others? All I ask is that I be placed near to likeminded individuals who also want to get on with their work.

4. Point: 'As a diligent young girl, I often feel resentful towards teachers who make me sit at a table with loud, misbehaving boys.'
   Evidence: 'Recent OFSTED reports … especially girls'.
   Explain: 'While I understand … get on with their work'.

75. Linking ideas

1.

Adding an idea	Explaining	Illustrating
Additionally	Consequently	For example
Moreover	Therefore	For instance

Emphasising	Comparing	Contrasting
Importantly	In the same way	Nevertheless
In particular	Equally	Alternatively

2. Extract 1 examples: therefore; consequently. Extract 2 examples: for example; however.

3. Answers will vary but all should use a P–E–E structure and feature a range of adverbials. For example:
   Fairs and festivals are a nuisance for local residents, causing disruption and distress. In particular, the noise from fairground rides – accompanied by the screams of children – keeps elderly folk awake late at night. Moreover, the litter that is left behind after an evening's entertainment is disgraceful. Consequently, fairs and festivals are an unnecessary and unwelcome addition to the community and the local council should prevent them from taking place.

76. Putting it into practice

Answers should be suitable for an adult audience and should include:
- a title
- an introduction
- details of the current situation and some appropriate recommendations

- facts/statistics to support the recommendations
- a conclusion.

77. Formality and standard English 1
1.
   - Conversation with friend: A, G
   - Conversation with stranger: C, F
   - Speech to scientists: D, H
   - Speech to peers: B, E
2. (a) <u>To Dave,</u>
   <u>It's okay for you</u>, wearing fancy suits and living in a posh house. What about poor nurses busting <u>there</u> guts for next to nothing? Just because <u>your rolling in it</u> doesn't mean the rest of us aren't screwed. It's just not right. <u>Me</u> mum says <u>your all bloody useless</u> and only look out for yourselves. <u>You need 2</u> sort it out.
   Advice could include:
   - be more formal in the way you address your audience – Dear Sir/Madam (or their surname)
   - don't be confrontational
   - avoid using slang
   - use correct homophones: 'you're' not 'your', and 'their' not 'there'
   - make sure that you use correct punctuation.
   (b) Answers will vary but should follow the advice given above.
3. Advice should include making it less formal. It could also include starting with a rhetorical question to draw in your audience, for example:
   Do you find yourself waking up even more tired than when you went to bed? Read our new article...;
   Want help holding back the yawns? Our newest issue will do just that...

78. Formality and standard English 2
1. 'Many adults believe ...' Both
   'I believe that skate parks ...' Both
   'Why do some people ...' Paper A
   'Kids ain't bothering ...' Paper B
2. For example: It would appear that everything young people do nowadays is a source of irritation for the older generation. **The youth of today are unfairly labelled as lazy, rude and lacking in morals. Why can't the more experienced and 'wise' citizens recognise that teenagers need a place to relax and socialise with their friends? It is time that these killjoys started to show some empathy for the younger members of their community.**

79. Vocabulary for effect: synonyms
1. For example:
   Everyone: the crowd, horde, masses, rabble
   Stared: gazed, glared, peered
   Shock: fright, dismay, distress, alarm
   Crazy: insane, mad, deranged, unhinged
2. For example:
   tired: Answers provided on page 79 of Workbook
   run: dash, scurry, sprint
   big: enormous, giant, monstrous
   tiptoed: crept, snuck, edged
   laugh: chuckle, giggle, snicker
3. For example: Looking back, it was the worst moment I'd ever experienced. I wasn't alone either. I was with **everyone in the whole park. It was truly the most humiliating day. The crowd peered at me like I was a curious animal in a cage, alarm on every face. They looked at me like I was deranged. All I wanted to do was scurry under a rock and hide before they started giggling at me.**
4. For example: Looking back, it was quite an embarrassing moment. At least I wasn't alone. I was with a handful of sympathetic people. It was a fairly embarrassing day. The people looked at me like I was an uncommon animal, with surprised expressions. I suppose I did seem a bit odd. It would have been nice to leave for somewhere I could be alone before anyone saw the funny side of it all.

80. Vocabulary for effect: creative
1. For example: The monstrous beast was standing before me **on paws as giant as dinner plates, and it swished its long bushy tail. As it growled, its snow-white fur stood on end, making it look even bigger.**
2. Answers should have focused more on the dog. The grass is not an important part of the scene and so does not need much description.
3. The description of the flowers is overwritten and so much could be cut. Parts also repeat meaning or state what is obvious, such as the 'wind blowing', 'randomly and illogically', the sun's warmth 'heating everything below it' and the loud sound of crickets 'making a lot of noise'. There could be further description of the beach, sea and the food (for example, the type of food).
4. Answers will vary depending on words chosen. They could introduce emotional feelings, or include literary techniques including metaphor, alliteration, personal anecdote or personification.

81. Vocabulary for effect: viewpoint
1. (a) Answer provided on page 81 of Workbook
   (b) Rubbish dumped **on the streets will still be rotting long after we are gone.**
   (c) Refusing to **sleep at a sensible hour means you will be exhausted the next day.**
2. misery: suggests people are unhappy about it, and sad that it's taking place.
   depression: suggests deep unhappiness – a serious problem with the issue.
   concern: implies there are worries about it, but not an emotional attachment.
3. Answers will vary but all should consist of two sentences and include vocabulary chosen for its impact and connotations. For example: Technology consumes every **waking moment, the never-ending, ceaseless ticking, binging and clicking that dominates our lives. Yet for many people technology can be a lifeline, an anchor to see them safe in stormy seas.**

82. Language for different effects 1
1. Rhetorical question: A, C; Contrast: D, F; Repetition: E; List: B
2. For example:
   (a) What qualifies **a person to vote?**
   (b) Voting, like driving, **needs a calm head, responsible attitude and a mature outlook.**
   (c) I am considered responsible enough to drive a machine that could kill but not to choose who represents me in government.
   (d) The right to vote, the right to have a say, is important to all of us.

83. Language for different effects 2
1. Answers will vary but answers could be:
   Many people drop litter.
   Direct address: Answer provided on page 83 of Workbook
   Pattern of three: People drop crisp packets, chocolate bar wrappers and even chewed gum.
   Alliteration: Loads of left litter lies on our streets.
   Some people play music loudly even late at night.
   Direct address: Would you want music pumping when you try to sleep?
   Pattern of three: Workers can't sleep, families can't talk and scientists can't even hear themselves think over the deafening music.
   Alliteration: The booming bass won't stop for a beat.
   Flying can be an uncomfortable experience.
   Direct address: You know that you've had at least one uncomfortable flight.
   Pattern of three: Between the tiny amount of leg room, the terrible films and sneezing passengers, the journey gets worse and worse.
   Alliteration: Forget flying, I hope to stay at home.

ANSWERS

2 (a) Answer provided on page 83 of Workbook.
(b) and (c) Answers will vary but could be:
The obnoxious person shouted into their mobile phone as if they were trying to be reach the caller's ears without it.
The obnoxious idiot screamed and hollered into their mobile phone as if they were a fog horn trying to signal to a boat at the other end of the sea.

3 Answers will vary but the final sentence might be too exaggerated, long or silly to use.

84. Language for different effects 3
1 A: Personification   D: Simile
B: Metaphor   E: Metaphor
C: Simile   F: Personification

2 Simile: It is as clear as **day that this rule discriminates against older teenagers.**
Metaphor: Children are imprisoned by **ridiculous rules on where they can go.**
Personification: The park gates smirk at older teenagers as they stop them from coming in to play.
Simile and personification: Older teenagers are as noisy as **alarm clocks but they still need a place to burn off energy; instead, they are made to feel unwanted by the cold and cruel hand of the law.**

85. Putting it into practice
Answers should include:
- language appropriate to the audience
- ambitious and effective language choices
- a range of language techniques, including figurative devices
- a consistent narrative voice.

86. Putting it into practice
Answers should include examples of:
- language appropriate to form, audience and purpose
- language chosen for effect
- figurative devices
- language techniques, such as rhetorical questions or patterns of three.

87. Sentence variety 1
1 (a) D: clause starts with a relative pronoun, such as 'which' or 'that'
(b) Answer provided on page 87 of Workbook
(c) C: clause is introduced by a coordinating conjunction, such as 'and' or 'but'
(d) B: clause cannot stand alone as a complete sentence
(e) A: Answer provided on page 87 of Workbook

2 For example: Firefighters, police officers and local charity workers, **all heroes in my opinion, work tirelessly every day for other people. Without a thought for their own safety, they risk their own lives every day. Comparing them with celebrity role models is a joke. No comparison! Their work is dangerous, while celebrity work is not.**

88. Sentence variety 2
1 Adverbs
2 Responses will vary but examples could be:
Pronoun: I was really unsure about it all.
Article: A nightmare was nothing compared to my first day.
Preposition: Next to an abandoned factory, the school did not look welcome.
An –ing word: Sighing, I made myself go to school.
Adjective: Sad, lonely and miserable. That's how I felt when she moved away.
A conjunction: If my friend is in all my classes then maybe it won't be so bad.

3 For example: Although I was usually **the first to get up and out of the house, something was making me drag my feet that morning. Slowly I spooned cereal into my mouth and chewed. I didn't feel ill but I didn't feel like myself. Climbing the stairs to get my bag, I tried to work out what was bothering me. The clock in the hall told me I was running late. Behind me the door slammed as I headed down the steps and on to the pavement. Speedy children dashed past me as I headed towards the bus stop.**

89. Sentences for different effects
1 The effect of the long sentence is that it emphasises the chain of events, and builds tension as the situation worsens. The effect of the short sentence is that it brings the scene to an abrupt end, focusing sharply on the narrator's horror.

2 The first sentence in text A emphasises **the dad's confusion at the narrator's unusual behaviour. Text B emphasises the narrator's plan to persuade their father to let them go. Note that the information the writer wants to emphasise usually comes at the end of the sentence.**

3 Answers will vary but all should aim to include a:
- long sentence followed by a short sentence
- sentence structured to give specific emphasis.

For example:
Recently, I watched all my neighbours lug brown bins to the end of their drives. As I walked past, I thought **about where these leftover items will go. In the landfill dump? Probably. Even if it is effectively disposed of, there are factories around the world pumping out more pollution than all the households in my street combined.**

90. Putting it into practice
Answers should include examples of:
- a range of sentence types
- sentences beginning in a range of different ways
- sentences structured for effect.

91. Ending a sentence
1 (a) .   (b) ?   (c) .   (d) ?   (e) !
2 For example:
(a) Answer provided on page 91 of Workbook
(b) How had he not noticed the hole in the boat before he set sail?
(c) The boulder gained speed, faster and faster, until it hit the wall with a terrific SMACK!

3 (a) B and C are correct
(b) For example: Sentence A is incorrect. This is a comma splice: two sentences are incorrectly joined with a comma. Sentence B is correct. The two sentences are separated with a full stop. Sentence C is correct. The two sentences are joined with a conjunction.

4 There are eight mistakes in total in the original, including the unnecessary exclamation marks at the end of the title:
The Cave of Doom [1]
I stumbled towards the gloomy cave. [2] Fear gripped me with its icy fingers and ran a fearful shiver down my spine. My skin began to crawl and sweat erupted around my forehead. What was this horrible place? [3] Could I bring myself to enter the mouth of hell? [4]
Turning back was not an option. [5] I had come this far and must enter this hateful hole. I held my nerve. [6] My head was spinning and my legs felt like they belonged to a different being. I called out in fear. [7] My words echoed across the darkness. [8] It was like listening to a large demonic creature.

92. Commas
1–2 A: Answer provided on page 92 of Workbook. Correct sentence: My favourite meal is cheeseburger and chips or spaghetti Bolognese; B: Correct; C: Correct; D: Correct; E: Correct; F: Incorrect: After working in a sausage factory, **[comma needed here]** my father never ate sausages again; G: Incorrect: The potato, **[comma needed here]** which is a good source of energy, should not count towards your five-a-day; H: Incorrect: Asparagus, **[comma needed here]** traditionally eaten with the fingers, **[comma needed here]** is in season from April to June; I: Correct

3 Answers will vary but all should aim to use commas correctly to separate:
- items in a list
- a main and subordinate clause – example provided on page 92 of Workbook
- a main and relative clause.

For example: Before the Smith family sat down for dinner, there were the usual arguments about homework. **The family, who lived in a large detached house on the edge of town, ate their evening meal at around 6pm each day. On this particular evening, Mr Smith had prepared a meal for his wife and their children, Paul, Mike and Isabelle. The atmosphere was tense. Mr Smith had recently been made unemployed, after 32 years with the same company, and was feeling angry, dejected and worried about the future.**

93. Apostrophes and speech punctuation
1–2 A: Incorrect: should be **don't**
   B: Correct
   C: Incorrect: should be **wouldn't**
   D: Incorrect: should be **dad's** because it is singular
   E: Correct
   F: Correct (plural: several girls' test scores)
   G: Correct
   H: Correct
   I: Incorrect: 'I'll get you for this, **[comma needed here]**' she hissed.
3 'So,' she began. 'Don't you think it's a bad idea?'
   'Aren't any adults going to be there?' he asked.
   'Of course there won't be!' She sighed, pulling her necklace where it had tangled in its chain.
   He thought about it for a moment. 'I don't see any problem with him going. It's not all night.'
   'Don't you remember what happened last time?' she pointed out. 'Don't you remember the broken window?'
   'Yes,' he admitted, but shrugged his shoulders like he didn't see its relevance. 'That was all of the students' fault, not just his.'
   'Or that his bed ended up in his best friend's pond?' He couldn't argue about that. His son's bed hadn't been easy to fish out of Sam's pond.

94. Colons, semi-colons, dashes, brackets and ellipses
1 Dashes
2 For example:
   (a) Answer provided on page 94 of Workbook
   (b) A healthy diet is vital: **[colon, followed by lower case i for it]** it can allow you to gain an edge over competitors who don't take care of their bodies.
   (c) Learning to be a good loser is essential; **[semi-colon, followed by lower case e for everybody]** everybody tastes defeat at some point. **[single full stop]**
   (d) I have always been good at the flute (since I can remember anyway) **[just brackets]** but wanted to be better.
   (e) Some cyclists take to the road without wearing a safety helmet – **[dash]** not a good idea.
3 I had left no stone unturned; the precious keepsake **[1]** was nowhere to be found. Vividly, I remember the day my grandmother (on my father's side of the family) **[2]** gave me this priceless family heirloom. For hours, I had scoured every corner of my bedroom – **[3]** even looking down the back of the dusty cupboards – but it still remained elusive. There was now only one place where it might be: **[4]** inside the bathroom. **[5]** Desperately, I rummaged through the washing basket **[6]** and searched under the cistern. **[7]** The only other possible location – **[8]** unless it had been taken in the night by the tooth fairy – **[9]** was the u-bend of the sink. I unscrewed the pipe, dragged out **[10]** clumps of mildewed hair and began to sift through the filth, looking for the glint of a diamond earring …

95. Putting it into practice
Answers should feature a range of punctuation used correctly, including advanced punctuation, such as colons and semi-colons.

96. Common spelling errors 1
1 (a) Answer provided on page 96 of Workbook
   (b) It was too soon to know what the **effect** would be on him.
   (c) It's not every day that you get to see one of those!
   (d) He was not **there** to help with **their** needs.
   (e) She saw what **its** problem was immediately.
   (f) **There** was nothing that would **affect** the problem.
   (g) It was **absolutely** and **scarily** out of control.
   (h) **There** was a large hill that **wouldn't have** been easy to cross.
   (i) 'It's bad,' he said **negatively**, 'they know where we **are** hiding.'
   (j) 'You shouldn't **have** said that **it's** true!'
   (k) We just hoped that **our** plan would have some **effect**.
   (l) Many students felt it had **affected** them **negatively**.
   (m) **It's** not the first time this has happened.
2 Answers will vary but should use a variety of the difficult to use words from Question 1.

97. Common spelling errors 2
(a) Answer provided on page 97 of Workbook
(b) She didn't know **whose** car it was that had sped **past**.
(c) The light switch was **off**.
(d) **Where** had he put the jacket he wanted to **wear** that night?
(e) There **were** two kittens in the basket, and a puppy **too**.
(f) '**You're** late,' she said, 'and you've lost your scarf.'
(g) I knew **of** him but he had never met.
(h) It was **too** hot; if they went jogging they might have **passed** out.
(i) They had been over there, but now they **were** behind him.
(j) **Your** other shoe is dirty **too**.
(k) **Whose** idea is this?
(l) **Who's** hiding in there and **where** is my purse?
(m) **We're** never sure **who's** off on holiday and **who's** stuck at school **too**.

98. Common spelling errors 3
1 Correct spellings are: argument, beginning, believe, business, conscience, conscious, decision, definitely, difficult, disappear, disappoint, embarrassing, experience, grateful, independence, occasionally, possession, recommend, rhythm, separately, weird
2 Answers will vary but could include examples like:
   Isn't it weird how the 'e' and 'i' in weird are alphabetical?
   It is embarrassing how greedy the word embarrassing is: it has to have double 'S's and 'R's.

99. Proofreading
1 Correct text is:
   • thing I've ever experienced
   • terrifying!
   • The views were superb
   • we'd plunge down
   • Moaning, whining, and then
   • distracted while driving.
   • pinpricks of light going past in the pitch black.
   • The quiet was deafening, but beautiful.
   • It was definitely
2–3 Answers will vary.

100. Putting it into practice
Answers should feature correct spelling, punctuation and grammar, and possibly signs of going back through the answer in order to make corrections.

Published by Pearson Education Limited, 80 Strand, London, WC2R 0RL.

www.pearsonschoolsandfecolleges.co.uk

Text and illustrations © Pearson Education Ltd 2018
Typeset and illustrated by York Publishing Solutions Pvt. Ltd., India
Commissioning, editorial and project management services by Haremi Ltd.
Cover illustration by Miriam Sturdee

The rights of Mark Roberts and Charlotte Woolley to be identified as authors of this work have been asserted by them in accordance with the Copyright, Designs and Patents Act 1988.

First published 2018

21 20 19 18
10 9 8 7 6 5 4 3 2 1

British Library Cataloguing in Publication Data
A catalogue record for this book is available from the British Library

ISBN 978 1 292 21373 6

Copyright notice
All rights reserved. No part of this publication may be reproduced in any form or by any means (including photocopying or storing it in any medium by electronic means and whether or not transiently or incidentally to some other use of this publication) without the written permission of the copyright owner, except in accordance with the provisions of the Copyright, Designs and Patents Act 1988 or under the terms of a licence issued by the Copyright Licensing Agency, Barnard's Inn, 86 Fetter Lane, London EC4A 1EN (www.cla.co.uk). Applications for the copyright owner's written permission should be addressed to the publisher.

Printed in Italy by L.E.G.O. S.p.A.

Acknowledgements
The authors and publisher would like to thank the following individuals and organisations for their kind permission to reproduce copyright material.
Page 007, 011, 012, 014, 016, 031, 043, 045, 046, 105: Copyright Guardian News & Media Ltd 2017.
Page 011, 020, 028, 039, 044, 047, 107: Copyright Guardian News & Media Ltd 2017.
Page 008, 024, 036, 101: Reproduced with the permission of Curtis Brown.
Page 118: Allen Carr's Easyway (International) Ltd.
Page 013, 019, 021, 029, 104: Reproduced with the permission of Don Congdon Associates, Inc.
Page 011, 019, 030, 032, 040, 042, 048, 109: https://www.thehistorypress.co.uk/articles/creating-ghost-stories/, ©Robert Hallman, by kind permission of the History Press.
Page 015, 102: "Chapter 1," and "Chapter 2" from THE KITE RUNNER by Khaled Hosseini, copyright ©2003 by TKR Publications, LLC. Used by permission of Riverhead, an imprint of Penguin Publishing Group, a division of Penguin Random House LLC. All rights reserved; "Excerpted from The Kite Runner by Khaled Hosseini. Reprinted by the permission of Anchor Canada/Doubleday Canada, a division of Penguin Random House Canada Limited"; © Khaled Hosseini, 2011, THE KITE RUNNER, Bloomsbury Publishing Plc.
Page 112: Excerpt(s) from THE GOD OF SMALL THINGS by Arundhati Roy, copyright © 1997 by Arundhati Roy. Used by permission of Random House, an imprint and division of Penguin Random House LLC. All rights reserved; Reprinted by permission of HarperCollins Publishers Ltd © 1997 Arundhati Roy.

Photographs

123RF: Songquan Deng 065; **Alamy Stock Photo:** Alexander Klenov 068, Maciej Bledowski 085, Jonathan Larsen/Diadem Images 095; **Shutterstock:** Antonio V. Oquias 051, Sam DCruz 059, Leoks 114

All other images © Pearson Education

Notes from the publisher

Pearson has robust editorial processes, including answer and fact checks, to ensure the accuracy of the content in this publication, and every effort is made to ensure this publication is free of errors. We are, however, only human, and occasionally errors do occur. Pearson is not liable for any misunderstandings that arise as a result of errors in this publication, but it is our priority to ensure that the content is accurate. If you spot an error, please do contact us at resourcescorrections@pearson.com so we can make sure it is corrected.